The author

Bernard J. Bienvenu is professor and head of the
Department of Management at the University of
Southwestern Louisiana. Dr. Bienvenu has contributed to five books, and his articles have
appeared in numerous business journals.

New Priorities in Training

New Priorities in Training

A Guide for Industry

Bernard J. Bienvenu

American Management Association, Inc.

Library of Congress catalog card number: 69–19435

First printing

To my students

Preface

IT IS READILY ACCEPTED THAT TRAINING MUST KEEP ABREAST OF, AND in fact ahead of, changes in worker qualifications necessary for effective employee performance. Most will agree that training, its objectives, policy, and practice, will not be as effective as it should be unless it results from a study of work—as it is now conducted and as it will be carried out in the years ahead—and unless such study be translated into worker requirements needed for effectiveness and be implemented by applicable training concepts and methodology.

Such is the objective and purpose of this book. Although it does discuss training methodology, its major emphasis is in the direction of analyzing the kind of work and qualifications demanded by the changing environment and how these should affect training. It also strives at developing an understanding of worker status, behavior, and changes in type of supervision, as well as advisable supervisory training, which both result from and are compatible with the new breed of employee. It examines job effectiveness, not only from the standpoint of skill requirements, but from many aspects of human behavior which affect employee performance. And it dwells on those special kinds of training problems—the disadvantaged, the dropouts, those in need of retraining, and so on—which emanate in large part from the same situations that impel a new focus on training and which also present a new and different kind of challenge.

The groundwork for this book was laid in 1960 when Paul

7

Grambsch, then Dean of the School of Business Administration at Tulane University, asked me to address a meeting of the New Orleans Area Chapter of the American Society for Training and Development. The major points of this paper later appeared in the November-December 1961 issue of *Personnel,* under the title, "What Kind of Training for Tomorrow?" During the past eight years, whenever the opportunity presented itself I have discussed training with personnel in industry, government, business, and education, as well as having conducted continuing library research on the subject.

It would be impractical to list all those with whom I spoke and whose thoughts and ideas helped in developing and refining the training concepts in this book. Many of the conversations were on a rather informal but most informative basis. I must particularly mention John Furr of the Ethyl plant in Baton Rouge, Louisiana, with whom I have talked training on numerous occasions during the past eight years. The training personnel of Boeing, Chrysler, and Kaiser Aluminum facilities in the New Orleans area were most generous in giving their time and in explaining their training philosophies and problems.

It is not only large industry that is troubled with the new worker qualifications demanded by the times and with what should constitute training. Charles Austin of the Austin Motor Company in Baton Rouge brought out so many questions and thoughts in just a few hours of conversation that it took me weeks to digest their significance. This is not to say that all those with whom I talked would be in complete agreement with what I have written, and of course I take full responsibility for the contents of this book.

The Dean of my college, Herbert A. Hamilton, has been a continuing source of encouragement in this endeavor, and he went out of his way in accommodating the special requests which were entailed in the writing and completion of this manuscript. His staff, Karen Bernard, Theresa Granier, and Janet Felps, rendered special assistance and were most patient with me during many trying periods. Hulda Erath and Doris Bentley of the faculty of the University of Southwestern Louisiana were very helpful in providing assistance and supervising clerical and secretarial tasks. Finally, my office staff, Jeanie Stein, Priscilla Daly, and Kenneth Broussard, all students, but professionals in dedication, work habits, and proficiency, helped and advised on the format, typing, and proofreading of the manuscript. And I must not forget the personnel of Dupré Library at the University, who, in spite of my impertinence, willingly fulfilled all of my requests. Lastly, I wish to express my sincere appreciation to the staff of the American Management Association, whose patience, persistence, and confidence in this project outlasted my procrastination.

BERNARD J. BIENVENU

Contents

1

The Changing Environment

FAILURE TO RECOGNIZE CHANGE AND TAKE INTO ACCOUNT ITS IMPACT on policies and on what needs to be given emphasis in the organization has, more than any other factor, resulted in difficulty in keeping up with the times. It has also brought about the diminution of competitive position and status, and it has often been the major cause of inability to survive.

Training is no exception to this axiom. It must pursue objectives and be administered in accord with the changing demands on the organization and its personnel. It can no longer be geared solely to the goal of preparing workers for immediate productivity; otherwise the organization will be faced with a never-ending retraining problem and an ineffective workforce. It cannot be the victim of tradition and have its efforts emphasize the needs of the past—or even the present—rather than the essentials for continuing effectiveness. It must be prepared to cope successfully with the many factors which have a bearing on productivity, rather than concentrating on job methodology in its artificial vacuum.

All this requires that training assume a different and more important status in the organization and structure its thinking and responsibilities to cope with the requirements of the new milieu.

The New Milieu

What is the new environment? How does it differ from the past? What is the impact of the new milieu on the various production processes and on particular industries and organizations? What kind of worker will be required? How can these new and different requirements be expected to affect training—its objectives, policies, plans, and programs? These are questions which must be answered as intelligently as possible by every organization if training is going to make the contribution necessary for adapting the worker—and thus the organization—to meet the challenges of the times.

Many industries have already entered a new era whose demands and characteristics are quite different from those of the industrial society in its traditional form, which, although a part of recent history, is now very much a thing of the past. The change in worker requirements is even more dramatic than that which occurred in moving from the agricultural to the industrial stage of development. Whether we call this new era the scientific age, the age of cybernation or automation, or any other name is nowhere near as important as is an understanding of the basic nature of the change. That many industries are moving from a skilled to a technical workforce (and one which requires mental competence and associated attributes) is clearly significant, but of far greater consequence is the recognition that this change is but a symptom of a more basic development. Most important is what has brought about this transformation: that is, the day-to-day discovery and accumulation of new knowledge and its practical application to various types of work, signifying the beginning of a change in emphasis from manual dexterity to mental aptitude. All indications point to a continuing acceleration of this change.

It is expected that requirements for professional and technical workers will increase by 54 percent in the period 1964 to 1975. Demands for the semiskilled and unskilled will continue to decrease, whereas it is anticipated that the white-collar group of employees will constitute 48 percent of manpower needs by 1975. And, when the rapidity of the change in work requirements and worker qualifications which has taken place over the past ten years is placed in proper perspective, it is feasible to conclude that the change in the workforce will be even more emphatic than present predictions indicate. Unmistakable in its meaning is the shift that can be observed within the percentage figures. What is presently regarded as skilled work in many industries and categories of occupations will probably move into the unskilled class, and the skilled employee will be supplanted by one in a higher hierarchy—the knowledge worker—who is not so skilled as he is analytical, technically up to date, and professional or semiprofessional in status.

Examination of the *Dictionary of Occupations* reveals that of the 23,000 different types of jobs in the United States, 6,000 did not even exist ten years ago. This significant creation of new jobs is merely an indication of changes in job types that can be expected in the years to come. For example, it is anticipated that by 1980 the metalworking industries in the United States will need some 200,000 "part programmers"—a classification that does not now exist. Manpower experts are concerned about the prospects of logarithmic jumps in our already highly developed industrial technology. They point out that such spurts will produce new jobs and outmode existing ones at a dizzying pace.

The merging of the sciences is changing significantly the concept of *skill*. It is, in fact, making the single-skilled technician obsolete. As the various scientific disciplines continue to become interrelated and interdependent, the worker will have to change accordingly and be qualified in the multifarious kinds of knowledge and skills which his work will demand. Already the job of electronics technician is taking on a new meaning—he must not only know electronics but must also be knowledgeable in hydraulics, mechanics, refrigeration, and other technical areas which are now involved in the jobs he is called on to perform.

Accomplishment, which once depended on the division of work into specific jobs and knowledge of a single repetitive task, is more and more becoming systems-oriented, and the systems themselves are undergoing continuous modification. Automation has decreased operator-type jobs and created a need for machine tenders and maintainers, and the complexity of modern machinery has forced a redefinition of the qualifications for the resulting jobs. And these are just a few of the many changes that are taking place in the makeup of work. Worker qualifications are being altered not only in jobs based on scientific technology. All work is being affected. Stock clerks must become inventory analysts, acquiring competence in computer systems; while mechanics, in progressing to instruments men, must bring to this new status an understanding of the jargon of modern electronics.

It is all this forward movement in worker talents and aptitudes which makes it difficult for the dropout and the disadvantaged to find gainful employment, and for the older and less educated worker to remain employable.

The New Worker

What will the changes accompanying the new environment require of the worker? What qualifications must he have in order to be productive and capable of meeting the demands which will be made on him? Such questions must be answered before any basic training theory can be devised.

It is often the case that training plans are developed before objectives and expectations have been established. This is usually due to a failure to analyze—and understand in depth—the environment in which the organization exists, its future course, the resulting job requirements, and the translation of these requirements into the worker qualifications needed for effectiveness. Even more serious, however, is failure to understand the advisability of moving away from job training to some kind of *worker training* which will provide a foundation enabling the employee to adjust as quickly as possible to changing work and occupational demands. For not only will changes be taking place within occupations, but, as Robert F. Mello of the U.S. Civil Service Commission states, "Six-year-old Americans now starting school can expect that their vocations—not their employers but their occupations—will change three times in their lifetime."

Adolf A. Berle, Jr. points out:

> To be employable, an individual must be skilled as well as literate. Literacy only establishes a base. The effect of increased mechanization is the progressive elimination of the need of "unskilled" labor—most (though by no means all) work that can be done by an unskilled laborer can be done by machine. This argues a need for further training in skills. But machines also are progressively displacing semiskilled and even highly skilled labor. This is the precise effect of "automation." Consequently, there is need for training above the literacy level—training in skills— which also creates a base permitting the individual to change from one skill to another.[1]

This makes it necessary that a basic objective of training be to instill in the worker the ability to adapt quickly, and with the least effort possible, in order to avoid retraining within an occupation and to minimize or eliminate retraining for new occupations.

Changes in job requirements and the frequency with which jobs are redesigned will place the worker in different work environments that demand of him not only technical adaptation but also skill in social and psychological adjustment. In some cases the importance of teamwork will be accentuated, while in others less human interaction and more individual responsibility will be required. Technical competence alone will not result in worker productivity unless the worker is prepared for social and environmental change in such a way that he is able to accept that change without affecting his willingness to work.

George Lombard describes the impact of such change on employees in the modern industrial organization:

> The people in Company X face ... questions at many levels. Knowledge has changed their products, processes, and markets. The engineers doing advanced development work are all under 30 years old. The pace of new knowledge in their area is so rapid that the knowledge of men who finished their education only 10 years ago is already out-of-date. Men who ran machines are now run by

[1] Adolf A. Berle, Jr., "Jobs for the Displaced: A Public Responsibility," in *The Great Ideas Today—1965* (Chicago, Encyclopaedia Britannica, Inc., 1965), p. 37.

them. Comparative oldtimers—the company is fairly new—who had bossed youngsters out of high school now find the latter telling them how jobs can best be done. Men who could not change their behavior had their jobs changed for them. To those who had struggled to maintain the belief that they were masters of their fate, this was perhaps the most wounding change of all.[2]

The development of the systems nature of work will require a conceptual knowledge of the total job to be accomplished rather than simply an understanding of, and competence in, a specific function within a system. Interdependence and interrelationships among the various task attributes which compose the system are major characteristics of this kind of work, and effective decisions and performance of a particular job in the system often rely on a comprehension of the overall body of work and the makeup of its many varied undertakings. Systems also undergo continuous modification, requiring new and almost never-ending change in the mental and technical qualifications of the worker. Conceptual understanding will also be of considerable help in providing a basis which will facilitate change from one task or occupation to another, and which will furnish a background permitting involvement in different systems with minimum retraining.

But the increasing need for the knowledge worker and the growing importance of multiskilled effectiveness, although significant, are not the major long-term demands on the workforce, for even multiskilled adeptness and contemporary job knowledge will be inadequate to cope with the problems of worker understanding of both theory and practice and the analytical expertise inherent in the increasing number of technologically and scientifically based industries and many other kinds of work once considered routine and mundane. Accelerated change and the upgrading of work now require a knowledge of the concepts of science, mathematics, and technology in which the work is grounded to insure lasting all-around competence and to minimize the arduous task of continuous retraining.

The math, science, and technology involved in modern-day jobs have in fact become one of the major means of communication while

---

[2] George F. F. Lombard, "New Directions in Human Relations," in *Management's Mission in a New Society*, edited by Dan H. Fenn, Jr. (New York, McGraw-Hill Book Company, 1959), p. 259.

at work. Unless these are understood by the workforce, it becomes virtually impossible to develop an understanding among the workers of what needs to be done. In automated industries, for example, where maintenance expertise replaces operator-type jobs, mathematics, physics, and blueprint reading have become required knowledge. The everyday language of work—and what was once clerical work —now demands the ability to converse in computer and programming terminology and the related technological languages.

Even background in the theory of mathematics, science, and technology will be of only short-term value unless the worker has the mental aptitude to build on his knowledge and to grasp new concepts as they are developed. The ideal, of course, would be to have a workforce so developed and entrenched in the nature of its work that its members would possess the perceptive mentality necessary to foresee change in their work and to understand its significance and relationship to the total task. Maintaining and expanding the mental aptitude and flexibility of the company workforce and bringing about some degree of perceptive mentality should be one of the major objectives of training and an important consideration in structuring the organization and determining corporate policy.

Workforce effectiveness will also require a change in the way the worker is looked upon by the organization, and a change in the way the worker traditionally looks at himself and the nature and scope of his work. A greater degree of independence and worker responsibility must become part of the makeup of the modern-day worker if the task of training and supervision is to be feasible and held within reasonable economic bounds. Many of the jobs already in existence and rapidly accounting for a greater percentage of the workforce require a worker change in attitude from that of dependence to independence and self-supervision; for the kind of work evolving very often fails to lend itself to established modes of supervision and requires the acceptance of greater responsibility by the worker. This is a dramatic change from the traditional view of the worker, by both the organization and the individual himself, as being dependent and requiring close and constant supervision. Instead of being simply an order taker, he will be required to take action on his own and use his own initiative and imagination to solve new and differing problems encountered in his work.

To avoid the difficult task of designing and maintaining never-ending retraining programs and the almost prohibitive costs which these entail will necessitate a more self-motivated type of worker. No longer will it suffice to limit training to the coaching traditionally provided by the supervisor and the instruction which takes place in the classroom. If this continues to be the case, the cost and time involved in keeping up to date the type of worker required by the new environment could become very burdensome. The new concept of training must find ways to develop within the worker the aptitude and motivation necessary to permit him to retain his proficiency in his occupation regardless of the changes in skill, knowledge, and ability required.

Much of what is today's kind of work is summarized in the following account of a father-son conversation, which is an excerpt from an advertisement published by the Pipe Council of Greater New Orleans:[3]

> *I have this thing with physics in school.* If it weren't for Dad, I'm not real sure I'd pass.
>
> I asked him how he got so good at physics, and he said it's because he uses it every day in his work. You see, my Dad's a pipefitter.
>
> You might ask, "Why does a guy fitting pipe need to know physics?"
>
> Well, I can answer that because I asked Dad the same thing. Architects and engineers work together to design big buildings such as schools, hospitals, office buildings, and industrial plants. Their designs include specifications for plumbing, heating and air-conditioning. Industrial plants have to move a lot of things all around their buildings: air, oil, chemicals, cleaning fluids and steam . . . lots of things that can't be moved any other way except through pipes.
>
> My Dad installs the pipes to do all these jobs. It takes lots of knowledge about many subjects, such as welding. Welding is one of the ways pipe is put together, so Dad has to be a good welder.
>
> Now, you might wonder what's so complicated about that. Dad said, "Let's take steam for example. Steam from boilers builds up

[3] *The Times-Picayune* (New Orleans, La., "Dixie" section), April 7, 1968, p. 11.

a lot of heat and pressure to the point where if you haven't used the right pipe and valves, the whole thing would not work correctly.

"Things like putting the pipes in the right places can take some figuring, too. You have to know how to read drawings and work out geometry problems.

"Then," Dad said, "there's processing, like the big plant we're working on now. There, the pipe's exposed to sun and rain, and . . ."

Demands on Training

Training is still looked upon as teaching a skill or task or increasing job proficiency. While this will always be part of the objective of training, its goal must also become one of finding ways and means of developing and enlarging traits which will be increasingly pertinent to satisfactory job performance. These traits are:

> The ability to adapt to change—technical, social, and environmental.
> The ability to change from mastery of a single skill to breadth of knowledge.
> The ability to change from singular to conceptual understanding.
> The willingness to be, not a follower, but a self-motivated individual.
> The willingness to give up being a mere order taker and become both imaginative and analytical.
> The open-mindedness to make the shift from dependence to independence and professionalism.

While it is true that automation sometimes makes certain jobs less demanding and less complex, emphasis on many of these traits will be necessary to provide the worker with the basic qualifications which will make him able and willing to change occupations. Neil W. Chamberlain, in writing on what the labor unions must do to adapt to what he describes as the "current asset revolution" (a term

which he uses to denote a present-day trend in union membership)
states:

> This tie to an occupation, the identification of one's *self* with a
> bundle of job characteristics, is part of the fabric of the economic
> society which is passing, and it will unquestionably complicate
> the asset management of a union official. Part of his problem is to
> induce in his members' minds the notion that in their lifetime they
> may have to develop new career lines, and sometimes change ca-
> reer courses, but that this possibility holds out promise and fulfill-
> ment as well as challenge and risk.

> The new approach to a person's career must in time supplant the
> increasingly romantic notion that a person *is* a garage mechanic or
> a postman or a newspaper reporter. It will not be easy to fix the
> idea that occupationally a person never *is*, in any continuing sense,
> but is always *becoming*.[4]

Industry must also be cognizant of this development and institute
measures to assist the employee in making the transition to this different way of looking at himself and his work. The result is that training
must be looked upon in a broader sense; its objective must be, not
only to increase worker know-how for the short run, but to provide
the training which will enable the worker to make necessary adjustments with the greatest possible ease and to increase his ability to
contribute to the organization from an aggregate point of view rather
than from the standpoint of his specific skill or job assignment. The
times require that the purpose of training shift from the single objective of increasing job proficiency to one of providing the basis for
day-to-day, long-run, *total* contribution to the organization.

The usual approach to training is to organize specific training programs to provide new techniques called for by changes in equipment
or changes in company product or process. Training is not looked
upon as a way of life by the organization; it is seen simply as a vehicle
to help solve an immediate and pressing problem. This concept of
training must now shift to the kind that will provide the traits which
will enable the worker to anticipate changes and develop the mental

aptitude and knowledge necessary to adapt readily to such changes. To accomplish this objective will require that training be looked upon as a continuous process. Refresher-type courses or training sessions designed to teach a new technique will become increasingly difficult to handle effectively unless the worker is kept up to date with advances and basic developments in the area of his skill or group of skills.

What is being advocated is an approach similar to the one that professional people must follow if they are to maintain an acceptable degree of competence. For, as worker qualifications shift from the physical to the mental, it can be assumed that the jobs of the knowledge workers in particular will more and more take on the characteristics of the professions. This should make the ultimate goal of self-training—shifting part of the responsibility for training to the worker himself—less difficult and within the realm of reality. But a change in expectations must first take place in order to provide the point of view which will permit self-training to emerge as an anticipated worker attribute. It should be recognized as a possible and desired goal and should require the development of an attitude which is conducive to the undertaking of this responsibility on the part of the employee. Indeed, providing the kind of environment and the motivation which will contribute to self-training should be one of the major considerations of training policy.

These demands on training may appear very difficult to fulfill on first observation, but the fact is that the worker of today is entirely different from his predecessor in background, education, and expectations. And each year that goes by will bring into the workforce a more capable and better-educated prospective employee. In the past ten years, the proportion of 16- and 17-year-old youths in school has increased from 75 to 88 percent, and the median level of education has risen from 10.9 years in 1952 to 12.1 years in 1962. Moreover, not only are the years of education on the increase, but significant advances have been made in the content of those years. So true is this that present-day graduates of many high schools have a better understanding of modern mathematics and science than many engineering college graduates of ten years ago.

Instead of looking at the new training requirements with apprehension, it should be recognized that the makeup of the modern-day worker and the work itself require this kind of approach. The new worker will demand that he be given adequate training. As Peter Drucker points out:

> ... The essence of the big change—and we are all past the midpoint in it—is not that we have to learn how to organize highly educated people for special work outside or next to the traditional business organization. The essential point is that tomorrow, if not today, more and more of the people in the normal traditional organization, in the day-to-day operations of a business, are going to be people with very high education; people who work with their minds rather than their hands; people who do everyday "line" work rather than special "long hair" work and yet who are different in their background, their expectations, and the way they work from the people who did these line jobs yesterday. . . .
>
> Their work is not physical, it is work of the mind. The only way to increase their productivity is to increase the output and the effectiveness of the mind. This can be accomplished only if we succeed both in making each of these men more productive in his own right and then in making this contribution more effective throughout the entire company.[5]

Impact on Corporate Policy

Although training has been given a great deal of lip service on the part of organizations, it is often relegated to a position of secondary importance and is usually looked at from a shortsighted and immediate viewpoint. And when cost-cutting programs are found to be advisable, the frequent result is the elimination of formal training divisions. Training departments have a tendency to be staffed by personnel who may not have been sufficiently competent in another area of corporate endeavor. Or they can become the place to assign employees who do not seem to fit anywhere else in the organization. In all too many cases the vocational school or some other type of public institution has been relied upon as the responsible body for training skilled and technical personnel for private industry.

The new breed of worker required by a large segment of business

[5] Peter F. Drucker, "Managing the Educated," in *Management's Mission in a New Society, op. cit.*, pp. 165, 169-170.

and industry today, the scarcity of skilled and technical workers, the inability of vocational schools to provide the types or numbers of needed workers, the advisability of continuous versus periodic training—all these point to the necessity of giving greater emphasis to training. It is reasonable to expect that workers will begin to associate job security and possibilities for advancement with training effectiveness. Companies which are known to have good training departments and policies will be given preference by the prospective employee and, consequently, will be more capable of attracting the better-qualified worker. Positive employee-management and union-management relationships will depend more and more on the emphasis given to training, and training will play a greater role in union-management contract negotiations.

Finally, as employees come increasingly to relate their economic well-being and their sense of dignity to up-to-date training opportunities, those employers whose policy gives greater importance to training will very likely be rewarded by high morale in the workforce. And, since such emphasis provides definite indications of employer interest, it should instill a greater degree of loyalty, resulting in increased worker productivity and minimum absenteeism and turnover.

It is not unrealistic to assume that contract specifications, particularly when government agencies are involved, will pay more and more attention to the training function and that employee development may soon be a major consideration in the decision of who gets the business. It is also reasonable to expect that government, in order to insure the availability of a competent workforce, may increase its interest in training to the extent of offering still greater incentives for its effective management and perhaps institute penalties when it is not given proper emphasis.

All of this points to training as a growing factor in determining productivity and profitability—one that will come to be recognized as an important aspect of social responsibility and a prerequisite to the economic health not only of the organization but of the nation.

2

The Training Process:
Introduction to the Job

L IKE ANY OTHER FUNCTION IN AN ENTERPRISE, TRAINING MUST BE
well planned if it is to be successful. But before the training
process itself is defined and developed, the overall objectives and
subobjectives of training must be determined. Conclusions must first
be reached on its purposes: on what needs to be and is to be accomplished by training. Failure to go through this type of thought process is one of the principal reasons why training plans often do not
produce results, and training effectiveness is very often difficult to
ascertain because needs and expectations have not been predetermined and, therefore, no standard exists by which to judge
results.

The basic objective of training should be to obtain from the employee *the maximum possible contribution*, from both a short- and
a long-run standpoint. It should be noted that this statement of objective moves away from the standard approach of simple job train-

ing to one which encourages and provides the basis for overall effectiveness and which requires that the training process concentrate on the worker rather than on the immediate job. Putting this approach into practice necessitates that training be considered under the following four headings:

1. Introducing the worker to the job.
2. Introducing the worker to the environment.
3. Instituting the continuous training concept.
4. Developing for total contribution.

Importance of Proper Orientation

The extreme importance of the first of these types, or aspects, of training is clearly apparent when we remember that the attitude which an employee develops regarding his work is strongly influenced by the way he is introduced to his job. Proper introduction provides an understanding of the nature and objectives of the work, what is expected of the worker, the relationship of the specific job to the total work process, the way in which the job is to be done, and so forth and so on—all of which leads to greater efficiency and productivity.

Although it would be difficult to disagree with the advisability of introducing the worker to the job in an appropriate manner, it is a part of training which is very often neglected. Line managers appear to relate productivity to being *on the job;* hence the desire to get the employee busy at the workplace as soon as possible. As a result, worker preparation is minimized and, in too many cases, given no consideration whatsoever. This leads to confusion and bewilderment on the part of the worker, is likely to have a negative effect on his attitude and productivity, and can be the cause of high worker turnover.

Dr. Harold P. Rodes, president of General Motors Institute, has commented on pre-job-assignment training and development as one of the major elements of a well-conceived training program. He says:

> Essentially this pre-job-assignment training is organized, or at least planned, preparation of an individual for a new or higher-level job. No longer is it practical to allow everyone to learn from on-

the-job experience what he needs to know to perform that job effectively. Because of the complex machinery and equipment with which many people work today, this method of learning it all on the job is certainly too costly. The increasing complexity of technical and management jobs demands certain minimal preparation of the individual before he is placed on the job.[1]

Case studies indicate that worker turnover and productivity are often directly related to job orientation. Poor introduction, or no introduction at all, leads to worker discomfort, frustration, and a feeling of insecurity which affects his ability to be cooperative and efficient. A disconcerting beginning can also establish an undesirable outlook and result in worker habits that will have a continuing negative influence on productivity.

The Case of Aaron Janis

A case situation will help illustrate the way in which the worker is very often introduced to the job and some immediate effects of failure to cover the advisable groundwork in training.

Aaron Janis, a high school graduate who scored above average on aptitude and intelligence tests, was employed by Martindale Electronics Company. Although relatively young, he demonstrated talents and ability which could, with additional experience, qualify him for a first-line supervisory position. He was first assigned to work in the resistor quality control section, but the company intended to shift him to different types of jobs in order to qualify him for supervisory work. Martindale was very much interested in young men of Aaron's caliber. It had recently been awarded additional contracts which would require a hike in production and an expansion of facilities. It was, however, short of the kind of men who could be advanced to the foreman level and was depending on the recruiting and training of young men of Aaron's type to provide the leadership and supervision necessary to meet the production goals to which it was committed.

Janis had worked for another electronics company for 15 months,

[1] Harold P. Rodes, "Evolving Models of Education for Progress." Reprinted by special permission from the August 1965 issue of *Training Directors Journal* (now *Training and Development Journal*). Copyright 1965 by the American Society for Training and Development.

but he had left this job because he felt that there was not much opportunity for advancement. He had also become concerned about his ability to keep up with the rapid developments in the field of electronics, since his employer provided only a short training period when he began work and had no program of additional training, and offered no assistance to its employees in keeping abreast of change. Janis had questioned his foreman about company policy in the area of training and was told that all he needed to worry about was meeting his daily production quotas. "Company policies are none of your business," said the foreman. "Besides, nobody bothered about my training when I was your age, and I made out all right." When inquiring about an insurance problem at the personnel office, Janis also asked about supplementary training and was informed that the company was thinking about this but that no definite plans had been developed.

Having been assured of the opportunities for advancement with Martindale, and feeling that he was going into an entirely different situation from his previous job, Aaron was looking forward to his first day's work with his new employer. He reported at the stipulated time —8 A.M.—going directly to the waiting area designated for new employees. After about an hour, a man whom Janis remembered having seen in the personnel office came into the room and asked Aaron if this was his first day on the job. He replied in the affirmative and was then questioned about the status of the four other men present in the room. Janis replied that he thought that they also were new employees, since they were there in the same room, but that he was not certain. The man then went to talk to these others and, after spending a short while with each one, left rather hurriedly.

A few minutes later, the following conversation took place between Janis and one of the other men, who introduced himself as Paul Hill:

HILL: Who was that?

JANIS: I don't know his name, but I'm fairly certain I saw him in the personnel office when I applied for a job.

HILL: Do you know where you're going to work?

JANIS: I was told I'd be assigned to the resistor quality control section. I wonder what this holdup is about?

HILL: I don't know where I'm going to work. All I was told was
to report at 8 A.M. sharp because the company expected
everybody to be on time—and here it is nine-thirty! I
wonder if we're going to get paid for all this time they're
keeping us waiting around?

At this point, a young lady entered the room and handed the men
their identification badges and work assignments. Hill told Janis that
he too had been assigned to resistor quality control.

HILL: Just what is quality control? I think I know what it means,
but I'm not sure.

JANIS: Well, at the last place I worked it meant testing the resistors to determine whether or not they were within the
tolerances allowed, but I'm not sure that the situation is
the same here. I suppose they'll tell us what it's all about
when we report to the section.

HILL: I take it you've had experience in electronics work?

JANIS: Yes, I worked for 15 months for a similar type of firm.
Most of my work was in assembly, but I was in the quality
control section as a replacement for about three days.

HILL: Man, I'm sure glad I met you! I don't know a thing about
this kind of electronics. After graduating from high school,
I went right into the army—I was discharged just the other
day. I guess they figured that since I went to radio operator
and maintenance school in the service I should be qualified to do this kind of work. I reckon we'll go through some
kind of program to let us know what we're supposed to do.

The two men began to walk around the plant area, looking for the
quality control section.

HILL: You know where we're going?

JANIS: I'm not sure. I wonder why they didn't tell us where to
go? Let's go by the personnel office and find out.

At the personnel office, Paul and Aaron were given a map of the plant
area. The building housing the resistor quality control section was
circled by one of the employees in the office after some deliberation

over its exact location. The site was finally determined by a plant worker who was in the office for an exit interview.

Hill and Janis arrived at their work at 11:30 A.M. They waited just inside the building for someone to tell them what to do next. After 15 minutes had gone by, Aaron approached one of the workers and inquired whether he knew who the supervisor was and where he could be found. The man replied that he had reported for work only three days earlier; he didn't know the name of the supervisor or much of anything else about the place; however, since the supervisor had already made his morning visit, he probably would not be back until the afternoon.

A few minutes later a whistle blew, the work stopped, and people started rushing off in several directions. Concluding that it was lunch time, Paul and Aaron followed one of the groups. They ended up in the lunchroom for employees who brought their noon meal with them and, after several inquiries, finally learned the way to the cafeteria. Although both were very hungry, they ate sparsely and hurriedly because they did not know how much time was allotted for lunch.

They returned to the resistor quality control work area and waited around for the supervisor. At 2 o'clock, he showed up and approached them.

SUPERVISOR: Are you the two new workers?

JANIS: Yes.

SUPERVISOR: Where in hell have you been? You were supposed to be here at eight this morning. We're already behind in our production, and without any output from you two this morning we're going to be 'way off.

Janis tried to tell the supervisor about the morning's events, but he was interrupted. "You're old enough to know you should have gone right to work without needing someone to tell you what to do." He then motioned to the stations they were to occupy and told them to get to work.

HILL: I thought the army was bad, but this place has got it beat. What am I supposed to do with this stuff? (*He points to the equipment at his station.*)

JANIS: I'm not sure. (*He picks up the ohmmeter and examines it closely.*) I worked with something like this for a couple of days once, but this one looks a little different. I'm not sure how it works.

HILL: Well, let's ask somebody.

So Janis and Hill asked one of the employees next to them how to operate the ohmmeter. The employee was upset by the interruption. He said he was already behind in his quota and, besides, it wasn't his job to train new people. Half a dozen other workers then gathered around the three and began to complain about the distraction. After the problem had been explained, Janis and Hill were given several demonstrations of the ohmmeter's use. Hill had a difficult time understanding the terminology, and he interrupted the men frequently in his efforts to find out what they were talking about.

With many questions still on their minds, Janis and Hill went to their work stations and began testing the resistors they found before them. Hill, uncertain of what he was doing, attempted to follow the procedure used by Janis. It was hard for him to learn the established way of using the ohmmeter, and he became so discouraged that in the end he just stood around doing nothing. He did, however, manage to incur the ire of some of the other workers, who eventually suggested that he leave the work floor if he just wanted to waste time.

Later in the afternoon, the supervisor came by and stopped to examine their production.

SUPERVISOR: Is that all that you've done? (*He follows this remark with others less printable, picks up an ohmmeter to check the new employees' work, and finds that many of the resistors do not meet the stipulated tolerances.*) And you've got the tolerances all fouled up. They told me you guys had had experience and would know what you were doing. What's been going on?

JANIS: I've had three days' work in quality control, but Hill here hasn't had any experience at all. Nobody was around to give us any instructions, so I just used the tolerances of the worker next to me.

SUPERVISOR: Can't you see by the color code that the resistors

> you're testing require different tolerances from his?
> How far did they dig to come up with you and your
> buddy?

The supervisor called two experienced workers to take over Aaron's
and Paul's work stations. Production had to be stepped up, he said;
the resistors were needed in assembly.

Aaron and Paul punched out and did not report for work the
next morning.

Lessons from Aaron Janis

The situation in which Janis and Hill found themselves is not
unusual. It is probably more typical than it is atypical, for introduction to the job is one of the most neglected phases of training and,
in most organizations, is not even considered to be part of the training process. Even when it is so considered, it is often looked at from
the very narrow viewpoint of simply training the worker in a single
skill and introducing him to a specific job, rather than providing him
with background knowledge of the total work and company
situation.

An analysis of the case of Aaron Janis brings out the following
important errors and omissions:

- Allowing the worker to report directly to his station without first providing him with background information and
  instruction regarding the job he is to do.
- Attempting to conduct on-the-job training in surroundings
  which do not permit adequate comprehension. The work
  situation made it almost impossible for Aaron and Paul to
  learn the job from their fellow workers—who constituted
  the only source of knowledge about the work open to them.
- Relying on inadequate and improper methods of instruction, which provide the bases for unsatisfactory production
  from the standpoint of both quantity and quality.
- Failing to introduce Janis and Hill to their superiors and
  fellow workers in such a way that a meaningful relationship, conducive to productivity, could be developed.
- Being unrealistic about worker response. Note that the

supervisor assumed that workers should be reasonably productive on their first day of work.
- Failing to inform Janis and Hill properly of what was
  expected of them and why it was expected.
- Making no effort to have the new workers understand the
  relationship of their job to the total task.

Paul and Aaron were not introduced to the workplace. The result
was considerable mental anxiety (which usually means decreased
productivity). They had no knowledge of where to go for lunch or
where to find the locker room. They were not made to feel that they
were part of the work group or the work situation; therefore, they
could not relate themselves to the other workers or relate their work
to other tasks. Uninformed as to proper communication channels, the
two were ignorant about how to get needed information and who
should be seen for answers to questions.

The supervisor, instead of trying to instruct Paul and Aaron in
terms understandable to them, attempted to make them improve by
showing them up. He failed to make sure that they knew the rules
of the workplace—what was or was not permitted. Perhaps he had
been told—or thought he had been told—that he was getting two
experienced men. However, prior experience does not necessarily
preclude the need for training, nor does it do anything to introduce
the worker to his new job from an overall viewpoint or to the new
environment, both of which may be different from that previously
encountered.

The company's failure to provide Hill and Janis with introductory sessions away from the workplace created conditions which
made it inevitable that they would distract other workers and
adversely affect the productivity of the group. Moreover, Hill's concept of the responsible employer was completely changed. He
became disillusioned, almost to the point of despair. Had he returned
to work, his enthusiasm and willingness to cooperate would have
been considerably lessened by his first day's work experience.

As for Aaron Janis, the work situation was entirely different from
what he had thought it would be. He too was disillusioned regarding his future with the company. This type of shock very often
results in rejection of the organization—even though the employee

does not resign but merely continues to go through the motions of working without really becoming a member of the team.

Objectives of Job Introduction

Just as the foundation received in formal education is a principal determinant of the ability to comprehend advanced subject matter and to progress according to established demands, job introduction should provide the basis for adapting to change and furnish the background necessary to enable the worker to not only become but remain proficient and productive. Introducing the worker to the job should therefore be looked upon much more from the long-range point of view than is presently the case. It should supply the skill, technical ability, and knowledge essential to the desired first-job performance, but it should also enable the worker to be a continuing asset to the organization, rather than a liability, when the first job becomes the victim of expected obsolescence.

Providing a proper foundation which will permit continuing adaptability and progress and insure competent first-job performance are, then, two of the basic objectives to be given emphasis in job introduction. A third objective is to take those measures which will enable the worker to develop a positive outlook as soon as possible regarding his job assignment, and to eliminate or minimize mental and psychological obstacles to productivity. Recent research findings indicated in one situation that

- The first days on the job were anxious and disturbing ones.
- "New employee initiation" practices by peers intensified anxiety.
- Turnover of newly hired employees was caused primarily by anxiety.
- The new operators were reluctant to discuss problems with their supervisors.
- Their supervisors had been unsuccessful in translating motivation theory into practice.[2]

2 Earl R. Gomersall and M. Scott Myers, "Breakthrough in On-the-Job Training," *Harvard Business Review*, July–August 1966, p. 64.

This makes it advisable that the training process include ways and means of enabling the worker to feel comfortable in his work and in the workplace. Thus inherent anxiety can be reduced so that maximum attention to, and concentration on, productivity is attainable as soon as possible.

It is well known that worker willingness and ability to be proficient are not determined simply by mastery of techniques, knowledge, or skill. Establishing meaningful relationships with fellow workers and supervisors and insuring familiarity with communication channels have a definite effect on the desire and ability of the worker to respond in accordance with expectations. Introducing the new worker to his human surroundings, clarifying the desired relationship patterns and available sources of information, and in general providing him with the knowledge he needs of the nontechnical and principally the behavioral aspects of the work situation therefore constitute the fourth major objective of introductory training.

Worker training should not only include new employee proficiency as a major goal. It should also be directed at minimizing the possibility of the beginner's having a negative effect on the attitude and output of those workers who are already on the job. Preventing such a situation from coming about, which is the fifth major objective of introductory training, requires that it be approached from the standpoint of group and organizational accomplishment of stipulated goals rather than simply from that of the individual worker as an isolated unit of productivity.

Implementing the Objectives

There is always a tendency to take things for granted, to assume that the new employee has certain knowledge and ability and is cognizant of the mores, traditions, and ways of doing things established by the organization. The work and the workplace, the existing relationships, the channels of communication have become an accepted part of the life of the employee who has been with the company for some time—so much so that he may suppose that these are common knowledge and hence overlook informing the beginner of many aspects of the work and its surrounding conditions which are basic to effective job performance. Supervisors, instructors, and training personnel have gone over the same information so often that it is mere routine. As a result, they (very often unknowingly) omit key points and procedures or fail to give proper emphasis to certain facts which are important to the trainee, and to his chances of reaching the desired degree of proficiency.

Nor should new employees be relied upon to ask questions in order to clear up areas of confusion, doubt, or ignorance. They naturally feel that they are going through a trial period and that their status is in jeopardy; therefore, they will refrain from giving any indication *which may appear to them* to be a threat to their job security. To the contrary, they may often respond to inquiries in a way that they think will denote knowledge and ability even though they may have neither and the questioner does not expect them to. It appears that a presumption on the part of the personnel concerned that Aaron Janis and Paul Hill had the necessary knowledge and ability for effective performance and understood the physical and human work arrangement with which they were confronted was one of the principal reasons for the company's failure to introduce them to their jobs properly.

Unless there is positive proof which leads to the conclusion that a different approach is advisable, it cannot be recommended too strongly that every effort be exerted to avoid assuming that the new employee has the knowledge of the job necessary for adequate performance. In no case should the importance of insuring full understanding of the workplace, working relationships, traditions, expectations, and other factors in the job situation be overlooked.

Providing for first-job proficiency. The case of Aaron Janis brings out many areas of weakness in job training for the beginner and points to the need for a more positive and formal approach. In fact, the Aaron Janis case is a classic example of what should not be done and of what needs to be accomplished.

First, the proficiency of the worker for the task he is to be assigned must be ascertained. This should be done by test or demonstration of ability, rather than by conversation; for, as previously noted, there will be a tendency on the part of the new worker to claim proficiency. It is important to guard against assuming the desired adeptness even in workers who have had experience in the job for which they were hired. The way in which such workers go about their work may not be the way in which it needs to be done.

Too, the same skill can have dissimilar implications and requisites in different situations.

Second, as much of the training as possible should be conducted away from the actual place of work, where—because of noise and other impediments to learning—it will be very difficult for the worker to gain the needed comprehension. Training at the work station can also result in embarrassing the trainee in front of his fellow workers—to the degree that it has a negative effect on his attitude and desire to produce. Moreover, it can, as we have seen, be very distracting to the experienced employees and thus have an undesirable influence on their rate of productivity.

The training method or methods used, the degree of intensity, the length of the training period, and the content and makeup of the training procedure should be determined by the ability of the new employee, the type of job to be learned, the skill and comprehension desired, and the overall company training objectives. And expectations should be firmly established. The worker should not only be told what is expected of him, quantity- and qualitywise, but should also be made to understand how and why the goals were established. The logic used in their determination should be explained, for an understanding of the reasonableness and validity of expectations helps to insure worker cooperation.

Then, too, the instruction should establish, on the part of the new employee, a thorough understanding and acceptance of the work rules. Failure to know what is or is not permitted can lead to the sort of frustration that is evidenced in the case of Aaron Janis. A mere verbal reiteration or printed listing of established regulations will not suffice; for, as with expected performance, compliance will result only if there is a true understanding of each rule's soundness, made evident by a valid explanation of the reasons for its existence and the purpose it serves. Of course, this presupposes that the rules have well-grounded and reasonable objectives and are not of the juvenile type that the modern-day worker finds very hard to accept.

The first move to insure work-rule acceptance should be the study of the regulations in force by instructors, supervisors, and others in authority. Not only should they know what the rules are, but they should also know why these are necessary, how they came about, how they are to be interpreted, what they are supposed to accomplish, how they have been changed by experience, how they are meant to be enforced, and what the penalties are for infractions. In essence, instructors and supervisors must agree on the advisability and validity of the rules if they are to get the employees to believe in them and abide by them.

Too often the reply to the subordinate's query, "Why is it this way?" brings about the answer, "Don't ask me, buddy—I just work here and do what they tell me. The people upstairs say this rule is necessary, and that's all that counts." The young men and women of today, because of their education and its relative quality, the sort of worldliness that is due to such factors as television, and the alternative job opportunities they know are available to them, are not likely to accept a framework of discipline and work conduct that is not based on logic and need. Their reaction to this type of response will probably result in lack of respect for their supervisors and other members of the organization, and it will probably stand in the way of their really giving what they can to their jobs. It may well start them to thinking, "If the people who have been working here don't know what's going on, and why things are the way they are, how can they expect us to be interested and cooperative? Maybe it would be better to look for an employer who cares enough to keep his employees informed and knowledgeable—a place where we can grasp the meaning of things rather than put up with all this 'Mickey Mouse' business. We've had enough of that in our lives already."

What must always be kept in mind is that we are not dealing today with the laborer mentality and temperament for which most rules and most training objectives regarding work rules were structured. Nor is the climate of the times what it was when most regulations presently in existence were instituted. The almost complete disappearance of the word "laborer" is striking evidence of this change, another aspect of which is the rebellion on college campuses directed at patterns of behavior expected by administrators and society. Both are strong indications of the demand for change in long-established codes of conduct. This kind of thinking is part of the mentality of the new employee, and he will not be effective or obedient in an environment structured according to past needs and for a different kind of worker. More sophisticated, intelligent, perceptive, inquisitive, using mental rather than physical attributes in his work, he functions best through understanding and reason. The normal practice of simply instituting regulations and commanding that they be obeyed will not bring the sought-after results. This is why proper indoctrination, with the goal of acceptance by reason, is more important now than it ever has been.

The study of rules by those responsible for devising, enforcing, and explaining them should not be a one-time affair. Rather, rules require perusal at least annually, to make certain that they are being understood and followed and to provide the knowledge necessary to insure proper interpretation and effective presentation to new workers. And it is also necessary, in this era of rapid change, that they be given an annual review to determine their continuing usefulness and applicability and to institute revisions, additions, and deletions that will bring them into accord with current needs.

After this basic step, the following means of gaining a favorable reaction and encouraging a spirit of compliance should be adopted where applicable:

1. The overall objective of the established system of expected conduct is the first thing to emphasize. The basic point to get over is that the purpose of regulation is to facilitate worker productivity and not to discipline. All rules should be viewed and explained in this context.
2. The rules should be discussed one by one with the workers, and stress should be placed on how each will help in getting the job done and making the environment more conducive to harmony and efficiency. It may be well to go into the situation which gave rise to each element of the code and show how its adoption remedied malpractice and discontent.
3. Examples of interpretation and accomplishment should be cited so as to make the rules seem more realistic and, at the same time, more significant and easier to recall.
4. It may be appropriate to have the rules explained by an experienced worker from the group to which the new employee will be assigned. This should help indicate acceptance by peers and thus bring about a greater degree of interest and acquiescence. It should also establish a fellow employee as a source of information to be contacted by the new worker whenever he is in doubt or in need of counsel.

The nature and complexity of the work situation may call for a review session devoted to rule analysis and understanding around the third month of employment. This step should be taken regardless of the apparent comprehension on the part of the new employee. The cost in time and effort required will be minor in comparison with the possible price to be paid if what appeared to be understanding does not really demonstrate itself in day-to-day behavior.

The tendency is to forget about work-rule acceptance when the indoctrination period is completed. But, as is almost always the case, rules change—or most certainly should change—as performance and environmental conditions are altered. The evolving nature of behaviorial concepts relative to productivity also makes it necessary to update codes of conduct. Whenever changes do take place, it becomes the responsibility of the training function to help bring about their acceptance—which of course entails a repetition of the relevant parts of this suggested procedure.

Providing a basis for long-term development. The necessity for retraining, the scarcity of needed skills, and the lack of sufficient numbers of multiskilled and knowledge-type workers can be the end results of looking at the employee from a short-range point of view. Workers who are assets to the organization often turn into liabilities when nothing is done by the employer to enable them to make the necessary adjustments to insure their ability to be continuously productive in their work or to master progressively increasing occupational demands. Although most young men and women presently entering the workforce usually possess the basic education essential for adapting to change, they are not too often provided with the means to keep up with advances in basic knowledge and theory which demand different or enlarged worker qualifications. Job introduction should begin the task of providing the background which will facilitate employee adaptability to new and changing work requirements.

The theory[3] behind the specific skill or multiskill should be

[3] Giving greater stress to theory not only is being advocated for industry but also is urged on education in general. Among many who have commented on this subject is John R. Bunting, who, in his article "What's Ahead for Business?" points out that the "incessant load of information emptying from the computer begs for more general intelligence in its use and interpretation. A more theoretical bent in education as opposed to our traditional pragmatic bias in this country would seem appropriate if we are to take full advantage of automation." *The Atlantic*, June 1964, p. 73.

brought to the attention of the new employee; and, in those instances where the job is based on the practical application of mathematic or scientific principles, a thorough grounding in such principles is recommended. This type of knowledge and understanding should give the worker the mental attitude necessary to look at the job in a more gratifying and meaningful manner. Comprehension of basic theory will be necessary for effective performance in an increasing number of jobs as the knowledge worker is called on more and more to make on-the-spot decisions regarding problems whose solutions require an understanding of the applicable theory.

A sound grasp of the basic concepts from which the work emanates should also provide the basis for coping with changes which take place in the nature of the job, since such changes usually come about because of a better understanding of the relative theory. As early as 1952, the United Nations Educational, Scientific, and Cultural Organization, in a study entitled *Education in a Technological Society,* stated:

> Up-to-date technical education, whether in schools, in industry, or both, is not sufficient to create an effective working force. Behind the technical instruction it is essential to have a sound general education even on purely utilitarian grounds. If there is not the underpinning of basic knowledge, no amount of training technique can get beyond a certain stage, while the possibility of readaptation, should the need arise, is greatly reduced.[4]

Related to theory orientation is the instituting of measures which will provide for proficiency in communication skills. The language of work, because of developments in theory and the changing nature of occupations, is very fluid. Terms which were used only one year ago may now be outmoded or have been replaced by new and different words. To begin to understand the nature and scope of the job as well as know how to perform it in an acceptable way obviously requires a thorough knowledge and comprehension of the terminology used in its conduct.

An excerpt from the 1968 Cadillac shop manual, presumably prepared for the guidance of automobile mechanics, will serve to illus-

---

[4] As reprinted in *The New Technology and Human Values,* edited by John G. Burke (Belmont, Calif., Wadsworth Publishing Company, Inc., 1965), p. 68.

trate the problems of present-day work terminology. It describes part of the composition and operation of the automatic climate control system as follows:

> ... The control system is composed of five major sections: three temperature sensors (thermistors) that sense the in-car temperature, the ambient air temperature and the discharge air temperature; a control panel that contains a transistorized amplifier and temperature dial; a transducer that converts an electrical signal into a modulated vacuum supply; the power servo unit that controls the vacuum circuitry to operate the system; and a circuit board in the power servo that controls the operation of the blower. . . .
>
> Whenever the engine is operating, the sensor string is transmitting a signal to the amplifier. The signal is converted to a proportionate DC voltage by the amplifier. However, the vent switch is providing a feed to the transducer. The transducer converts the electrical signal to a proportionate regulated vacuum output that is supplied to the vacuum power unit of the power servo, thus placing the power servo unit in the maximum air conditioning mode.

This kind of rather complex description, far from being an exception, is more nearly the ordinary way of characterizing many of today's jobs. It also points up the dramatic leap in qualifications necessary to be an automobile mechanic—a job that is still thought of as based on physical and mechanical requisites but now demands judgment, analysis, mental expertise, and other attributes typical of the knowledge worker. It brings out in an obvious way the fact that a higher literacy level, with a knowledge of theory and applicable terminology, is much more essential today than it was just a few years ago—even for the so-called automobile mechanic, who must now really become an instruments man.

Yet it is not only the understanding of the task which requires a good grasp of terminology, but also the changed nature of many occupations, demanding interpretation, analysis, and—very often—conference and group-type decisions and work. The ability to communicate effectively therefore becomes one of the prerequisites of employee adaptability and work-group efficiency. What must be kept in mind is that in many situations the ability to communicate effectively, and to comprehend the communication media in use, is equally as important as knowing how to do the work.

For example, the change from the mechanical to a more highly scientific, technical, and sophisticated type of engine and accessory equipment, and from the simple to a complex and sensitive kind of engine performance, has created vexing problems in automobile agencies and repair shops. In one case, a graduate engineer was on hand to interpret the shop manual in such a way that the "mechanics" could understand the language used and the methodology of repair. In another situation, the owner and the shop superintendent, both of whom had a good education and considerable experience, acted as diagnosticians. In both instances, dissatisfaction was expressed regarding the procedures in use. Communication and comprehension problems necessitated continuous work stoppages to answer questions and explain how the work was to be performed, and the need to rework jobs a second or even a third time was not unusual.

Dr. Ida Hoos stresses the significance of communication in these words:

> Communication skills within the organization itself or in relation to the world around us are important as never before. Human intelligence is required in the generating of ideas and in the expression of them. Technology can merely spread them. And the worth of such dissemination depends entirely on the value of the original thought.

> Herein lies a mandate for all training executives. Whether soap or sonar equipment be the end product of a firm, production workers and clerical staff, supervisors and management must be encouraged to improve their language skills. A high degree of literacy may well turn out to be the prime asset in our computerized age. This becomes increasingly apparent as routine functions are done mechanically and the task of interpretation gains importance.[5]

Devising a program to assure knowledge of needed terminology and develop the ability to communicate in accordance with the

[5] Ida Hoos, "Retraining Accomplishments and Challenges—Profit or Waste?" Reprinted by special permission from the August 1964 issue of *Training Directors Journal* (now *Training and Development Journal*). Copyright 1964 by the American Society for Training and Development.

demands of a specific occupation becomes a prerequisite in many cases for proficiency at the workplace, and in such situations it should be an integral part of training plans. Some guidelines to achieving these goals are as follows.

The first step is to determine the comprehension of terminology, the language skills, and the communication methodology needed for expected performance. This requires a detailed study of the way in which the job is done and the human interaction which takes place. It also necessitates a study of the job itself. For example, routine work will demand less literacy than the kind that varies and is linked to differing instructions or is analytical in scope. Job descriptions should not be relied on solely for this purpose, since the way the work is actually performed can depart significantly from the formally prescribed method. Also, it is often the case that changes and advances in the nature of the work take place more rapidly than it is feasible or possible to change the job description. This makes it advisable that a review of literacy and communication requirements take place at least annually and that testing and in-struction materials be updated accordingly. Otherwise what is tested and taught will not be what is actually taking place.

Second, new employees should always be tested for the pro-ficiency desired. Probably the best type of test is to present an actual work-problem type of situation and ask trainees to describe in their own words how they would handle it. This is the most realistic way of ascertaining literacy and knowledge of terminology. The employee can respond in the media in use on the job—either written or spoken—so that his communication skill can be judged as well.

Those who meet the requirements can then be sent to the work-place for further testing. The supervisor or some other person should be designated to judge terminology comprehension and communi-cation skill on the job. After a trial period, the worker can be certi-fied as capable from the standpoint of these qualifications or can be assigned for additional training. This training should alternate with actual work in order to gain the benefits of combining classroom and on-the-job learning.

Courses of instruction should be set up for the workers who do not meet minimal proficiency requirements. After grasping basic terminology, students should undergo a laboratory or simulation-type learning period for purposes of realism—as well as to suggest the variety of job situations and the different communication skills and terminology required with each set of conditions to which they will be exposed. This should not be a cursory kind of learning experience but should be well thought out. New employees can be very much embarrassed, and impede the effectiveness of other workers, if they do not have the required level of terminology comprehension and the competence necessary to communicate in the manner expected.

After workers have been on the job for a stipulated period—two months or more, for example—a review discussion should be scheduled to clear up any possible terminology and communication questions or weaknesses, since the employees concerned may be reluctant to admit on their own to what they may consider personal inadequacies. The training officer should obtain the information he needs from supervisors or experienced workers in the same group. This will furnish a positive basis for structuring the conferences to insure maximum effectiveness.

In addition, some system should be devised for upgrading basic language and communication ability for those new employees who are deficient in this respect as determined by the testing procedure. Courses can be developed by the training department, local trade-school or college offerings can be utilized, or it may be that correspondence courses will serve the purpose. Preferably, employees should be permitted to use company time to take such courses, and the employer should bear part or all of the costs. It is important, too, that the employer provide some incentive, create the desire to undertake such study, and furnish the sort of guidance that will help assure continuing effort.

The relationship of the specific job to the total work process should be an integral part of the introductory program in order to develop a basis for long-term adaptability. The worker can hardly develop an appreciation of the significance of a particular job unless he can relate what he is supposed to accomplish to the end product. As the interdependence of different tasks becomes more and more the rule, effective decision-making ability will be possible only if there is an understanding of the total job and the relationship of its parts. This type of comprehension is particularly important in those industries which are subject to rapid change, for worker proficiency in a specific task will be determined by more than ability to adjust to changes in the task itself. Rather, it will require an understanding of all aspects of the total process to insure that any change will be coordinated with the various work elements. The interrelationship of various tasks is so significant in some areas of work, particularly those of the systems type, that it would be very difficult if not virtually impossible for a worker to adapt successfully to technical and scientific changes in his own job unless he understood what was going on around him.

There are several ways through which this can be accomplished, and in many companies efforts are being directed at developing a total work understanding on the part of the employees. But such an effort can be so narrow in scope that it fails to meet the objective of really relating one's work to the total process and demonstrating the significance of the individual contribution. Simply showing the worker a movie of the overall work plan and its integral parts, or a model of the production process, is certainly advisable; however, it does not go far enough toward developing the comprehension that is desirable. Rather than a one-step formula, a *procedure* should be sought that will enable the worker to *live* within a concept of his occupation and its overall purpose. Such a procedure might include the following training suggestions:

1. New employees should be assembled to hear and participate in a discussion of the origin, nature, and basic purpose of the total task. The historical development leading to the present process might be described so that the work to be done can be envisioned in its proper perspective.
2. A model of the system, which can be used to point out the important phases of the work flow and significant jobs within each phase, can then be used to give the employee a visual and mental understanding of the overall objective and the part played by each work element involved.
3. This demonstration can be followed by a movie of the total production procedure and its different aspects so that an action image can be supplied. The movie should not only concentrate on the pertinent system but relate it to the end product.
4. A walking tour of the system, including an explanation of the functioning of its integral parts, is another recommended step.

5. Finally, a discussion-and-answer period should be scheduled to ascertain the degree of understanding established and to clear up any possible misconceptions. At this time, the system can again be described and a summary given of its major components. The work supervisors and group leaders should be present to answer inquiries and provide additional information, as well as to better orient new employees to the human aspects of the work process. If it is done tactfully, so as to avoid possible embarrassment, novices may be asked to write out their understanding of the total work process, its objectives, and their own role in it before the session convenes. This will establish a basis for the discussion and give some idea as to what information may have been misinterpreted or not understood as desired.

Much of the foundation for long-term development will depend on the degree to which the employee is led to comprehend the nature and the significance of his work. For example, Professor Otis Lipstreu concludes, "The traditional skill concept has centered around manipulation and experience. The new skills appear to be related more toward the accumulation of technical understanding, and perhaps to the development of basic abilities such as awareness, alertness, and increased attention span."[6] Most training, in contrast, stresses memorizing the procedure necessary to perform the immediate job rather than developing the thought process. As a result, the mental outlook of the worker is very often one of extreme rigidity rather than flexibility, and his receptivity to new ideas and new ways of doing things is dulled. The ability to qualify for new and differing job demands, and the attitude and mental framework needed to facilitate a change in occupation with minimum cost and effort, will depend very much on the way in which the worker is taught at the very outset of his working life. Training must shift from concentrating on memorization to encouraging individual thought and discovery. Letting the worker think things out, find the answers for himself, should be utilized to provide the needed flexibility and so structure the mind that learning new techniques or even changing one's occupation completely will be freed from much of the difficulty presently being encountered. The earlier a person is trained in this way, the more likely he is to develop the traits that will provide the basis for continuous adaptability and productivity.

As one authority has stated, ". . . much of the knowledge today's students will need hasn't been discovered yet, and much of what is now being taught is (or may soon become) obsolete or irrevelant. What students need most, therefore, is not more information, but greater depth of understanding and greater ability to apply that understanding to new situations as they arise."[7]

Relieving tension and anxiety. Whether or not it is apparent, almost all new employees will experience a considerable degree of anxiety. Questions concerning adaptability to the assigned task, the right behavior, the need to adjust to new personalities, and many other problems will be occupying the mind of the new worker. Much the same doubts, moreover, will also be plaguing the worker who has changed jobs, even though he has been with the organization for some time. And it is very difficult to achieve the expected degree of comprehension and needed concentration unless these questions and doubts are relegated to the background as soon as possible. Consequently, an important objective of introductory training is to minimize the anxiety that is natural in the new or transferred employee and relieve him of the frustrations which can hinder the learning process and so endanger productivity.

Considerable stress can result from failing to explain work procedures and requirements in a way that is understandable to the employee. The language used by the instructor or supervisor may involve an unfamiliar vocabulary or require a level of comprehension that is beyond the trainee. The situation is made worse by the fact,

---

[7] The same author's comments on programmed learning also are of interest: ". . . And the small steps and the rigidity of presentation and limitation of response make a degree of boredom inevitable, at least for students with some degree of creativity.

"If programming is used too extensively, moreover, it may prevent the development of intuitive and creative thinking or destroy such thinking when it appears. For one thing, programming instruction seems to force a student into a rather passive role, whereas most learning theorists agree that no one can really master a concept unless he is forced to express it in his own words or actions and to construct his own applications and examples.

"More important, perhaps the rigidity of structure that seems to be inherent in programmed instruction may imply to students that there is only one approach, one answer; yet what the students need to learn most of all is that some questions may have more than one answer or no answer at all." Charles E. Silberman, "Technology Is Knocking at the Schoolhouse Door," *Fortune,* August 1966, p. 123.

already pointed out, that a new employee will very seldom indicate by asking questions or by attitude that he does not understand the work procedure being described or the instructions being given him. Also, the trainer's familiarity with his subject may lead him to cover significant points too hurriedly.

Every effort should be made to insure that instruction is within the realm of worker understanding. Nontechnical, simple vocabulary should be emphasized, and the jargon of the trade and of the workplace should first be defined before it is used to describe the procedures to be followed. Repetition of important points which have caused difficulty in the past should help to alleviate the dangers of hasty and cursory coverage. Trainers should on occasion verify their presentations for comprehension, by giving them to peers or others who are unfamiliar with the material covered and then testing for assimilation and for areas which can lead to confusion or fail to produce understanding. Too, both comprehension and freshness are often aided by going through the whole process of thinking through the content and method of one's presentation and possibly restructuring and rewriting it. The longer a particular set of instructions is used, the more likely it is no longer achieving the desired objectives and can be significantly improved.

The first days of training should be as relaxed as possible, and an informal atmosphere should prevail. Pains should be taken to foster congeniality among the workers and between the workers and the trainers. The aim should be to give the trainees confidence in themselves, instill in them a sense of security, and alleviate natural fears regarding the work and the workplace. An orientation procedure utilized effectively by Texas Instruments furnishes a guide to success in this area. It emphasizes the following four points:

1. *"Your opportunity to succeed is very good."* Company records disclosed that 99.6 percent of all persons hired or transferred into this job were eventually successful in terms of their ability to learn the necessary skills. Trainees were shown learning curves illustrating the gradual buildup of competence over the learning period. They were told five or six times during the day that all members of this group could expect to be successful on the job.
2. *"Disregard 'hall talk.'"* Trainees were told of the hazing

game that old employees played—scaring newcomers with exaggerated allegations about work rules, standards, disciplinary actions, and other job factors—to make the job as frightening to newcomers as it had been for them. To prevent these distortions by peers, the trainees were given facts about both the good and the bad aspects of the job and exactly what was expected of them.

The basis for "hall talk" rumors was explained. For example, a rumor stated that more than one-half of the people who terminated had been fired for poor performance. The interviews disclosed the fact that supervisors themselves unintentionally caused this rumor by intimating to operators that voluntary terminations (marriage, pregnancy, leaving town) were really performance terminations. Many supervisors felt this was a good negative incentive to pull up the low performers.

3. *"Take the initiative in communication."* The new operators were told of the natural reluctance of many supervisors to be talkative and that it was easier for the supervisor to do his job if they asked him questions. They were told that supervisors realized that trainees needed continuous instruction at first, that they would not understand technical terminology for a while, that they were expected to ask questions, and that supervisors would not consider them dumb for asking questions.

4. *"Get to know your supervisor."* The personality of the supervisor was described in detail. The absolute truth was the rule. A description might reveal that the supervisor is strict, but friendly; his hobby is fishing and ham radio operation; he tends to be shy sometimes, but he really likes to talk to you if you want to; he would like you to check with him before you go on a personal break, just so he knows where you are.[8]

Establishing a knowledge of relationships and communication channels. The case of Aaron Janis illustrates the quandary in which the new worker often finds himself and the effect which failure to

[8] Gomersall and Myers, *op. cit.*, pp. 66–67.

develop an understanding of the human aspects of the work situation can have on the attitude and productivity of the employee. Janis and Hill were lost; they did not know where to turn or whom to approach for answers to the many questions which are typical of what one should expect from a new employee. Even when training is given more serious consideration than was evident in the company which employed Hill and Janis, it often concentrates simply on job technique and procedure; it very seldom gives the worker an awareness of the existing community that he will have to work with and the accepted codes of behavior.

The worker should be introduced without delay to those individuals who are qualified to answer questions in areas of interest to him, particularly about subjects which affect productivity. The process of introduction should involve more than simply mentioning the various people by name. Ideally, the experienced workers, supervisors, or personnel department representatives should talk to the newcomers and attempt to anticipate those inquiries which they know from experience will come up and which are of immediate concern. Also, they should try to develop an atmosphere which will permit rapport between the workers and those who are responsible for their performance and can keep on improving it.

Some effort should be made to convey an appreciation for the traditions, standards of conduct, and effective relationships established by the workforce in general and particularly by the group that the worker will be directly associated with. In essence, the worker should be told what the group will permit, what it will frown upon, and what it likes and dislikes from a behavioral standpoint. In all probability, the immediate supervisor will be the best-qualified person to furnish this information.

The new employee should be introduced to those people with whom he will be working, particularly those with whom he will be closely associated and fellow employees whose positions are such that they can have a positive effect on his productivity. This includes the immediate supervisor, members of groups who perform related work, and key employees who are recognized as productivity determinants because of their standing in the group. Their personalities should be described in a way that will furnish a basis for understanding how to establish effective rapport with them and enable new employees to relate themselves to their supervisors and fellow workers in a way that is conducive to productivity. Opportunities should be provided for the new man to talk informally with the immediate supervisor and with fellow employees, and questions about the work and the workplace should be encouraged. All this should take place before the worker reports to his station so as to avoid the type of situation that arose in the case of Aaron Janis.

Minimizing possible negative effects on productivity of fellow workers. Very often overlooked is the possibility that the introduction of a new worker into an established situation can influence the existing attitudes and outlook. Also, the inability of the new employee to reach the expected level of productivity can weaken the desire of other workers to be proficient. In group-type work, output can be impaired when the novice cannot perform his work at the pace necessary to keep up with established standards. Or failure to fit in with accepted behavior patterns can result in being ostracized or, in more serious instances, can lead to open or quiet rebellion on the part of those who belong to the constituted order. The point to emphasize here is that all reasonable precautions should be taken to avoid such occurrences and their damaging effect on productivity.

When an organization can be selective in recruiting management trainees, the ability to fit into the organization is one of the major criteria used, and this characteristic also is emphasized in the development of prospective management personnel. But this trait is very seldom given attention in recruiting and training at the worker level. What must now be kept in mind is that the nature of work in many industries, and of the worker himself, has undergone considerable change; therefore, the relationship problem—although ever present—has become of still greater significance among the rank and file.

The ability to adjust to a new environment should in fact be given as much attention as selectivity permits in the recruiting of the knowledge worker, and his training will have to stress this qualification increasingly. This will not be as easy as it first appears, for although the type of behavior desired and accepted at supervisory and management levels has been studied and fairly well defined in many organizations, very little knowledge has been accumulated on this subject as far as the worker group is concerned.

The first-line supervisors and the workers themselves should be of assistance in furnishing data which will be beneficial in providing guidelines for recruiting and training. Foremen's training should give emphasis to their responsibility for seeing that recruits learn the accepted behavioral patterns and to the advisability of keeping in close touch with the new worker during his first few weeks of employment so as to help him make the adjustment required to fit into the group to which he is assigned. With the changing demands on the workforce, requiring of the rank-and-file employee more and more of the traits expected of management, it can be reasonably assumed that the same behavioral characteristics presently looked for in candidates for management positions and stressed in management development will be increasingly called for on the worker level.

Providing new employees with the necessary knowledge of relationships and communication channels, as described in the preceding section, should do much to minimize the possibility of their being a drawback to the productivity of other workers. Also, when at all feasible, the prevailing degree of proficiency should be required of new employees before they are assigned to their workplace. This is particularly advisable in those cases where the new workers are to be assigned to already established group-type work. Inability to meet worker expectations of productivity, so that the group is prevented from meeting its normal goals, can seriously affect morale and result in an attitude which is damaging to worker desire to be efficient and to maintain the customary competence. Where satisfactory performance cannot be insured before the actual work begins, training should at least provide the basis for reaching the established goals within a time period which is acceptable to the workers who are already on the job.

3

The Training Process:

Introducing the Environment

I NTRODUCTION TO THE ENVIRONMENT IS GIVEN VERY LITTLE ATTEN-
tion; in most cases, it is not even considered to be part of
training. The strong desire to get the worker to the workplace as soon
as possible very often results in simply a cursory review of the environment in which the new worker will find himself. Also, there is a
tendency for training and supervisory personnel to look at the task
of orientation principally from their own viewpoint, rather than
from that of the new worker; therefore, they fail to give this important subject the attention which it deserves. What they overlook
is the significance which employees attach to this topic; the fact that
mental confusion or inability to understand the surroundings and
conditions of work will definitely have a damaging effect on worker
attitude and productivity. Rather, those responsible should look at
this phase of instruction with an eye to answering the questions and

solving the problems which are important to the worker as well as conditioning him to their own and the company's expectations.

Introduction to the environment should emphasize company policies and procedures, familiarize the newcomer with the physical surroundings, provide an understanding of the new milieu and its demands on the worker, and orient the individual to the expectations of the organization and the requirements of the times.

Understanding Policies and Procedures

What happens if I am ill? Whom do I call? What is the policy of the company regarding other types of absences? Are there any provisions for retirement? Will my employer help me to keep up with the changes which take place in my skill? What are the rules of discipline and the penalties for violation? What are my chances for promotion? These are but a few of the many questions which will be nagging the employee when he first becomes part of the organization, and the sooner that such questions are answered the more likely he will be able to devote his full attention to job performance.

Obviously, failure to clear up these natural queries will make it very difficult for him to concentrate on his assigned work. Moreover, unless the organization takes an active role in making certain that the needed type of information is provided, the new man will, of necessity, rely on other members of the workforce as sources of knowledge. And such reliance can very often lead to the communication of hearsay, rumor, or just plain misunderstanding—what is thought to be the situation rather than how things really are.

In the absence of definite arrangements to insure comprehension of policies and procedures, the overwhelming likelihood is that the new worker will be misinformed, for he will be receiving his information from others who—like himself—have never been provided with the real facts. There is no doubt that considerable confusion, mistrust, and lack of confidence in the employer, all resulting in reduced productivity and poor attitude, can stem from employees' ignorance of company policies and procedures. They may think and act in accordance with what they assume to be right, but the "rules" turn out to be guidelines made up by the workforce for lack of authoritative information from the employer.

One of the objectives of indoctrination is to make the employee feel that he is part of the organization and that the employer is concerned with him as a person. This is rewarding to both the organization and its employees. Consequently, it is the usual practice to use the first day of employment to develop an understanding of policies and procedures on the part of secretarial, clerical, management, and other white-collar personnel. But the blue-collar or skill-type worker must in most cases be satisfied with a brief pamphlet which attempts to develop an awareness of what is very often complex material—information that is not easily understood when presented in this manner. It is only natural that this group of employees should feel slighted and begin to develop the attitude that they are somehow separate from the rest of the company; for, in truth, this is the way they are being treated. Instead, it should be recognized that the knowledge worker, who is accounting for an increasing percentage of the workforce, is more nearly in the white-collar category and regards himself as having the same status as other personnel. To treat him differently risks damaging his pride and his willingness to be cooperative and productive.

No training program is really complete unless it includes ways and means of insuring an understanding of company policies and procedures. But, even when this is acknowledged, the desired results may be thwarted because the material which is presented may be regarded by training or supervisory personnel as being of significance to the worker but may not really satisfy his questions. Also, unless the teaching method really develops an understanding rather than simply making the worker memorize the material, the intended goals will not be achieved. The first step, therefore, is to determine the real areas of concern. This can be done by placing oneself as much as possible in the same frame of mind as the new employee and thinking out problems that may be troubling him. Questions which come up during the first months of employment should be noted and answered during the indoctrination program; for these same queries will surely be important to new employees in general —and the sooner they are answered, the sooner the worker will be able to give maximum possible attention to his work.

Understanding rather than simply memorizing must be the goal in mind if the organization is to achieve the real benefit of policy and procedure orientation. This means that the logic and reasoning behind the rules must be presented in such a way that their necessity will be accepted. Unless those who are subject to them understand the need for their existence, cooperation and obedience will be wanting. The discussion method—and encouraging questions rather than simply lecturing—is more likely to insure the desired degree of awareness. And, since policies and procedures are very often subject to varying interpretations and one may take precedence over another, examples of their practical application should be emphasized in the learning period to assist in gaining acceptance. In cases where it is difficult to cover all the areas involved, the new employee should be introduced to a fellow worker or supervisor working in his vicinity who has the necessary knowledge and willingness to respond to questions in an intelligent way.

Familiarization with Physical Surroundings

Perplexity and bewilderment on the part of the newly hired can be the result of failing to acquaint them with their physical environment. This is evidenced in the case of Aaron Janis. Aaron had very little knowledge of his surroundings and was really in the dark regarding his work station. As a result, he was not as effective at his work as he could have been, he wasted time, and his concentration was unavoidably directed away from the task he was assigned to do. To feel that one is part of an organization, and that the organization is concerned with the well-being of its members, is a natural desire of most people. But it is difficult to see how this beneficial attitude could result under the conditions in which Aaron Janis was thrown into his surroundings. He clearly felt that he was more of a stranger—and more unwanted—late in the day than at its start.

As is the case with policies and procedures, the usual company outlook regarding familiarization with physical surroundings is somewhat paradoxical. It is generally accepted practice to introduce all employees other than those in the worker category to their surroundings. The first few days at work are usually spent touring the premises and trying to make the new employee feel at home. That this same type of treatment would assist in gaining the cooperation of the rank-and-file plant worker and help him to become productive in the shortest possible time is very seldom seriously considered.

What is overlooked is that this group of employees have very much the same feelings and sensitivities as any other job holders in the organization. To repeat: With the increasing level of education in our society and the upgrading of skills and jobs, the gap between white collar and blue collar is narrowing, and it is reasonable to assume that long-established distinctions between various classifications of employees will continue to undergo change and to lose their former significance. It is already evident that the knowledge worker enjoys a higher·status than his predecessors—indeed, he appears to be on the brink of gaining a position where he will be second only to management in importance in achieving the organization's goals.

Acquainting all employees with their physical surroundings, and making certain they are furnished with the tools necessary to do their work, should do much to alleviate the anxiety and bewilderment of the new man and should be regarded as an important aspect of the training process. In this way management will not only provide the knowledge necessary to minimize worries and frustrations but should also help in developing an attitude of belonging to, and being an integral part of, the organization. It will demonstrate the concern for the new employee felt by the representatives of the employer and aid in eliminating or forestalling the "they don't care attitude" that is too often prevalent in the thoughts of the worker regarding management.

As time goes on, and as the worker category of the organization is composed more and more of knowledge-type employees, these individuals should be regarded as being very much on the same level as other higher-status classifications of job holders with like attitudes and desires. They will have to be ministered to in accordance with this change in status if they are to make an effective contribution to the organization. Certainly this is the way in which the knowledge workers themselves will look at the situation, and they will expect the same treatment as has traditionally been given to employees in the white-collar classifications.

In any event, a better understanding of the assigned task will result if the employee not only is acquainted with his immediate physical surroundings but is given the opportunity to develop an awareness of the entire plant and its operations and to familiarize himself with the location of its various divisions. And there are many ways in which this can be done. It may be that the familiarization process in use for other classifications of employees is adaptable to the knowledge worker. A suggested training procedure to acquaint the employee with his surroundings might consist of the following:

1. The first day of employment, or part of it, can be devoted to developing a sense of the background and history of the organization. A movie or presentation slide will probably be the best method to achieve this purpose; but, when neither is available, a lecture combined with some other type of visual training aids can be used. Paradoxically, plant visitors are usually offered such a presentation, but it is not often utilized for new employees. Yet it would appear that this can be a good means of developing worker interest and making newcomers feel more at home in the enterprise.

2. The company's organization structure should be presented in a general way, after which there should be a somewhat more specific discussion of the plant setup. The function of the local offices that are of special interest to the new employees—such as training, personnel, and insurance—should be emphasized.

3. An explanation of the plant's purpose and its overall method of operation will be helpful in providing an understanding of what is going on and how the different procedures—including the work of the employees concerned—fit together to form the whole. A film or flow charts can be used to implement this phase of orientation. However, it is important that questions and discussion be encouraged, thus providing still another way of insuring a greater degree of comprehension.

4. Next there might be a tour of the plant complex, with the instructor giving a verbal description of the operation and relating his account of it to the preceding steps in the orientation process. The location of offices and areas of special interest should be pointed out. If feasible, a walking tour will probably best serve the purpose of establishing the geography of the plant, particularly in relation to the area where the employee is to be working.

The new worker is now ready to be acquainted with his own place of work and the facilities provided for his comfort and well-being.

Establishing Expectations and Insuring Knowledge of Milieu

The desire to be productive is determined in part by the expectations which are established; moreover, the willingness to devote time and effort to keeping abreast of change is influenced by one's awareness that such discipline is necessary and advisable. John Gardner states:

> The relation of education to the level of motivation in the society is more direct than most people recognize. The goals the young person sets for himself are very heavily affected by the framework of expectations with which adults surround him. The educational system provides the young person with a sense of what society expects of him in the way of performance. If it is lax in its demands, then he will believe that such are the expectations of his society. If much is expected of him, the chances are that he will expect much of himself. This is why it is important that a society create an atmosphere that encourages effort, striving and vigorous performance.[1]

Although this quotation applies specifically to education, all indications point to its general applicability. There is considerable evidence to signify that expectations can play an integral role as a productivity determinant and as a motivating factor which encourages the effort necessary to insure continuing adeptness. Much of the success of many organizations is due to a certain spirit which creates a willingness in its members to strive to excel. This attitude is very often present because it is *expected*. As Gardner states in an earlier work, "If there are no expectations, there will be little high performance."[2]

Creating an environment which is conducive to high perform-

[1] John W. Gardner, *Self Renewal* (New York, Harper & Row, 1963), p. 20.
[2] John W. Gardner, *Excellence* (New York, Harper & Brothers, 1961), p. 101.

ance on the management level is one of the principal objectives of many companies. In those organizations where this is accepted management philosophy, great effort is devoted to instilling this concept in the management trainee; and, very often, the theory of so-called "management by objectives" is given steady application. But this whole idea of expectations and the resulting effect on productivity is not often considered to be applicable to the lower echelons of the company. In fact, the worker is frequently thought of as being lazy, noncooperative, anxious to get away with as little work as possible, and unwilling to invest the time and study necessary for self-improvement. He finds it very difficult to become anything but what he is expected to be.

An integral aspect of training should therefore be directed at insuring worker understanding of company expectations. Very often the worker is blamed for failing to meet established goals when he has not been informed of them. This is not simply a question of verbal communication, although explaining company and departmental goals to new employees is the first step in the right direction. The reasonableness of established expectations *must* be acknowledged by those who are to abide by them. This requires that they be just, well thought out, and within the reach of the individual employee.

A positive viewpoint on the part of training and supervisory personnel is highly important. They too must be convinced that the desire to accomplish—and, in fact, accomplishment itself—very often results from their own outlook and the attitude which they relay. It is impracticable to expect positive results from employees if they are looked at apprehensively by training and supervisory personnel, for any worker will reflect and act in accordance with the existing environment as he sees it and senses it to be. The impression communicated, intentionally or unintentionally, at the beginning of the work experience has much to do with shaping worker attitude and influencing the contribution he is willing to make to the organization. Since the first significant contact with the company is usually with the training department or with the immediate supervisor, both play a vital role in developing the desired worker outlook. The responsibility for training in this area should therefore not only focus on the new employee but also be directed at instilling in supervisory personnel the desirability of positive expectations.

Failure to remain proficient in an occupation, or to adapt to needed change, is usually the result of inability, inadequate knowledge, lack of desire, and the difficulty which the individual finds in personally coping with the problems he encounters unless he is given guidance and assistance. There is not much that can be done about basic inability, and creating desire can be a trying task, particularly when the lack of it reflects incurable laziness. But training can be instrumental in insuring that employees are continuously aware of external developments affecting their skills and changes in the nature and value of their work. Thus no introduction to environment can be called complete unless it includes plans to foster worker understanding of the new milieu and brings into being on the part of the worker a sincere appreciation of the demands and challenges that will confront him. It should also include a thorough explanation of procedures and methods instituted by the company to provide the needed direction and assistance.

In short, the impact of the new milieu on worker effectiveness should be anticipated in such a way that the employee will gain the confidence necessary to accept the inherent challenges realistically and be fully assured of company direction, aid, and cooperation in meeting them.

4

The Training Process:
Continuous Training

MOST TRAINING IS BASED ON THE CONCEPT OF SATISFYING A SPECIFIC and very often immediate need or alleviating a known deficiency. Generally it is looked upon from the standpoint of a tailored program designed to fulfill a definite, singular purpose. Also prevalent is the assumption that the greatest degree of learning occurs at the workplace—that is, while operating the machine or during actual work performance. It is these three criteria which very often determine the development of training plans. There is no intention here of questioning their past effectiveness; no doubt they will remain applicable for certain industries and types of work and continue, in even the most modern of industries, to play a part in the training function. But it is also apparent that the new type of work and the new type of worker require a different training emphasis, and that training fundamentals which were once applicable will not be sufficient in many industries and organizations to insure a capable workforce with the knowledge, skills, and other qualifications necessary to meet the challenges of the new industrial environment.

The increasing role of the knowledge worker; the rapidity of the technological changes and advances in knowledge which necessitate a continuous redefining of skill and competence; the growth of the systems concept; our growing dependence on science; the constant redesigning of jobs and job requirements; and the elimination and addition of occupations—all these require that training assume new and different perspectives if the worker is to be prepared to cope successfully with the changing requisites for effectiveness. They give added emphasis to the fact that training must concentrate on the worker rather than on the job, for training will become an increasingly difficult task unless the worker is ready to adapt to the new demands being made on him.

The need for frequent staging of tailored programs can be an indication of failure to adopt and implement a training philosophy which is consistent with the times. It will be too late to handle training effectively if it takes place only when a specific need arises, for the worker in all probability will not have been given the opportunity to develop the background needed for adequate response and adjustment. Work that requires more mental aptitude than physical dexterity is not the type that can be learned on the job unless it is preceded by training which allows for the development of the necessary background and attitudes. Thus our three criteria—that training must meet a specific need, that programs should be designed for a particular reason, and that learning is most likely to occur on the job—while long the cornerstones of training success, must now become secondary to the concept of *continuous training*.

Continuous training has as its objective that of furnishing the basis which will make for worker readiness to adjust to change with the least possible cost and with minimum effort. Neil W. Chamberlain describes the situation in these words:

It has now become an article of faith among manpower specialists that there is no place in the modern world for the uneducated and the untrained. But there is only a tenuous difference between the uneducated and the undereducated, the untrained and the undertrained, and once we admit that in most occupations knowledge runs ahead of the pace at which a worker can keep up with it, we are driven to find some means of providing for our continuing education throughout our lives.[1]

Chamberlain emphasizes the impact of change:

To exaggerate only slightly, it is highly unlikely that the tool-and-die maker completing his apprenticeship today will ever again possess as much *relevant* knowledge as he has now. The exaggeration can be wholly removed by saying that at some point early in his career his competence to deal with the new and developing technologies will be subject to steady erosion.... We are still operating as though a person can acquire in the first twenty years or so of his life all the formal education he needs to keep him on an ascending career line through the remaining 40 years or so of this working life. But the fact is that the clock starts running down the moment a young man or woman steps from the commencement platform, be it college or high school.[2]

The objective of continuous training can be implemented only if there is a right-about-face in the way in which the worker is viewed. It cannot be stated too often that he is not the same as the worker of the 1930's and bears very little resemblance to the worker of the 1940's or the 1950's; that he is closer to the professional classification than he is to the blue-collar category and certainly does not look at himself as does the traditional blue-collar employee. The more highly educated product of a better environment who is oftentimes more knowledgeable about his work than his foreman, he performs a different type of work—a type which carries with it a degree of respect and reverence heretofore almost nonexistent. He will be productive only if he is treated in a manner which is appropriate to his new status and the image he has of himself.

This new worker cannot be trained in the traditional way if he is to maintain the desired degree of proficiency—simply because he and the work that he is performing are not part of that tradition. More and more, as has been stated, his work is taking on the

[1] Neil W. Chamberlain, "Retooling the Mind," *The Atlantic,* September 1964, p. 49. Copyright © 1964, The Atlantic Monthly Company, Boston, Mass. 02116. Reprinted with permission.
[2] *Ibid.*

characteristics of a profession, and this requires that his training be of the type which is best suited to maintaining professional competence. As is the case with the professions, he cannot really be trained in the true sense of the word, but must be furnished with the incentive, direction, tools, and environment which will permit him to undertake, on his own, the greater part of the effort required to keep up with developments in his work. Some principal avenues for providing him with this help are:

- Scheduling discussions by employees of work changes and developments.
- Providing means for grasping fundamentals which are the foundation and source of the work process.
- Making library resources available and establishing ways of encouraging their use.
- Promoting professional associations of knowledge workers.
- Taking advantage of special situations which furnish opportunities for effective training.

Scheduling Employee Discussions

Knowledge workers should be permitted to assemble at planned intervals (the frequency of the meetings to be determined by need and resulting accomplishments) to discuss changes and developments in their work. These meetings should be on a regularly scheduled basis and should take place during working hours. Not only must it now be recognized that learning is as much a part of work as is the actual work itself, but the time spent in learning is in fact becoming more significant than that which is occupied with actual production. For, in more and more cases, the end results will be possible only if preceded by the acquisition of pertinent knowledge. The selected topic for discussion should be announced ahead of time so as to give the participants the opportunity to give some thought to it, and a discussion leader with a thorough knowledge of the subject should be present to insure proper guidance and to act as a source of knowledge.

It should be emphasized that the discussion and its direction should be left as much as possible to the participants and that the

leader should inject himself into the proceedings only when necessary. The goal of such gatherings is to have the workers themselves
analyze the subject, examine the problems which it presents, and
come to acceptable conclusions about its significance and implications. A second purpose is to give more responsibility to the worker
and to train him to analyze and think for himself. He should then
be more proficient on the job in that he is able to figure out solutions to different problems himself rather than having to call for
assistance.

The advisability of this new direction in training is brought
out in the UNESCO treatise entitled *Education in a Technological
Society*. One of its conclusions is:

> Many of our difficulties today are caused by the fact that students
> do not learn how to think, or to do and find things, for them-
> selves—which should be the first aim of all education. Too much
> emphasis is laid upon the communication of second-hand informa-
> tion which is apt to stay in the pupil's mind only until examination
> time. No solution of the problem of reorientation of general edu-
> cation can be found, therefore, in merely adding new subjects to
> an already overburdened curriculum. A new way must be found
> of teaching the basic subjects as they exist, a way which lays
> stress not merely on the student's ability to benefit by reading,
> but also on his capacity for using his eyes and hands and for
> cooperative enterprise, whether in the workshop, the theatre, the
> school camp or the playing field. . . .
>
> What is required is not so much a new kind of curriculum
> (although this may be necessary) as a new kind of teaching;
> and with it a new kind of aim in education—the fitting of the
> young person to master technology, not merely to become one of
> its cogs. . . .[3]

The discussion leader, therefore, should be more of a guide than
a director of the conversation, and the degree of success of this
type of learning experience can usually be judged by the lack of
necessity for participation on the part of the leader. The more the
participants intelligently discuss the topic on their own, the greater
the degree of accomplishment.

[3] As reprinted in *The New Technology and Human Values,* edited by John G.
Burke (Belmont, Calif., Wadsworth Publishing Company, Inc., 1965), pp. 69, 71.

Although the subject for discussion should be preselected, this should not preclude the consideration of related or other significant topics that are on the minds of the group's members, provided that airing them may be beneficial to the members' work. General topics which should be considered for this phase of continuous training are:

1. *Industrywide changes.* These might be discussed every six months or so. The implications of present and expected future developments and their effect on the course of the industry could provide stimulating and rewarding discussion. Minds should be stretched by encouraging reasoned speculation and short-term, intermediate, and long-term prognoses of industry direction.

2. *The effect on skills brought about by changing product makeup and new developments in industry* as well as expected and future shifts in the skills themselves. This should be a good follow-up topic. It may be advisable to assign it for discussion at a specified future date as a way of terminating topic No. 1 on a positive note and leaving the participants with something to think about. One way to start this session might be to have the participants write up changes which they forecast will take place in their occupations, the reasons for their beliefs, and the ways in which they expect to prepare for them. The prepared papers, embodying predictions and suggested methods of preparing to cope with skill transformation, can be read to the group and serve as a good basis for discussion.

   The discussions can also stimulate company thinking regarding training needs and advisable plans and help inculcate a reasoned sense of direction in training policy. Recognition of the need to consider and introduce special courses of study designed to upgrade skills may emerge from such sessions. In fact, the provision of a means by which the organization will be able to determine the direction in which skills are moving, the ability of employees to cope with these developments, and the type of action appropriate for the organization to pursue may be the most significant outcome of these learning periods, since no formal method of analysis in this area appears to be in use at this time. That the problem of changing skill requirements is already with us in some fields and rapidly approaching in others is evidenced by the following determination on the part of the National Manpower Council:

> Many of today's electricians will have to learn electronics if they are to retain their skilled status. Pipefitters may have to learn hydraulics. A skilled worker who formerly measured with calipers and now uses a micrometer will soon have to learn to work with tolerances measured with light waves. . . .

3. *Production, organization, behavior, training, and other problems with which the company is faced* and which involve the employees. Worker deliberation of these situations should provide for a deeper understanding on their part of management's involvement and could be of considerable help in determining acceptable courses of action. Such discussion broadens the learning base of the workers and gives them a feeling of participation and usefulness.

4. *Circumstances in different parts of the organization which require a change in the way of doing things.* These are appropriate subjects for discussion when they are germane to some aspect of the participants' work. The nature of a particular situation, the way in which it was handled, the decisions made, the lessons learned as a result, and the applicability of all these factors to other occasions and company areas should provide stimulating material for thought and self-expression and should have a positive effect on productivity.

It should not be concluded that the concept of continuous training confines itself to industry, skills, or technical developments. Any subject which can affect productivity, or which represents a new viewpoint or advance in thinking and is related to performance, should be given consideration. New discoveries in motivation, behavioral theory and its applicability to different work groups, emerging ideas on communication, new personnel regulations and practices, changing conditions within the organization, economic aspects of the work situation, developments by competitors—these are all subjects which can add to worker comprehension, awareness, flexibility, and adaptability.

Affording an Understanding of Fundamentals

Continued work proficiency is becoming more and more dependent on a knowledge and understanding of the fundamentals which form the basis for a skill or occupation. To be able to cope with change requires a good grasp of the developments which are taking place in the theory of the work; and this, in turn, demands an appreciation and comprehension of the underlying principles involved. John Gardner states:

> Nothing contributes more damagingly to the unemployment of educated talent than rigid specialization and rigid attitudes supporting this specialization. . . . If technological innovations reduce the demand for his specialty, he has nowhere to go. On the other hand, if he is broadly trained in fundamental principles and knows that he may have to apply those principles in varying contexts over the years, he is in a position to survive the ups and downs of the job market.[4]

Rather than specialized education, Gardner suggests:

> The alternative—and the wiser course—is to educate men and women who are capable of applying excellent fundamental training to a wide range of specific jobs.[5]

Since this concept of education is not generally followed, business will have to provide the training which will permit the worker to adjust to changing work demands. Even when the worker's background is exceptional, it will still be advisable for the organization to offer the guidance and assistance which will facilitate an understanding of basic theory and new developments. This can be

[4] John W. Gardner, *Excellence* (New York, Harper and Brothers, 1961), p. 43.
[5] *Ibid.*

accomplished by sponsoring courses and classes in the applicable subject matter. For example, a comprehension of the principles of advanced mathematics and science is becoming increasingly pertinent to effective job performance in many industries. What must be recognized is that dramatic and rapid changes are continuously taking place in these subjects, and that the worker must be given both direction and the opportunity to remain abreast of the basic knowledge he requires in order to remain proficient.

Those responsible for training should set up regularly scheduled learning periods which focus on new concepts and their application and should encourage the review of pertinent theory. This type of learning experience should keep the participants' minds active in the subject-matter area so that they will be continuously capable of grasping changes quickly as they take place. Jacques Ellul, in *La Technique*, brings this point out rather forcefully when he states:

> It is possible, if the human being falters even momentarily in accommodating himself to the technological imperative, that he will be excluded from it completely even in his mechanical functions, much as he finds himself excluded from any participation in an automated factory.[6]

It may be of value here to reemphasize that workforce effectiveness will depend on the acceptance of the concept that the most productive aspect of work will be the time spent in learning, and that the organization should make available during working hours the time necessary for keeping up with change and furnish the proper guidance to help insure fruitful results: that is, an up-to-date worker, capable of "accommodating himself to the technological imperative." It is also worth reiterating that the greatest and most lasting degree of accomplishment will be attained if the method of learning is one which promotes a type of environment that will encourage the worker to think things out for himself as much as possible. This will help guarantee the type of comprehension that permits the application of available theory and the use of ingenuity and imagination rather than simply the performance of a specific task in a set way.

[6] As quoted in Don Fabun, *The Dynamics of Change* (Englewood Cliffs, N.J., Prentice-Hall, Inc., 1967), Part I, p. 26.

Making Provision for Worker Use of Library

The installation of a plant library and the encouragement of its use by the knowledgeable worker can be an important avenue of continuous training. Having available, close at hand, the basic and most respected periodicals dealing with current thought and dis- coveries and their industrial applicability should at least make information accessible which, if studied, should contribute signifi- cantly to worker effectiveness. Reading lists and reading plans should be devised, and personnel should be induced to make use of them along with the library.

Although probably it would be difficult to achieve, consideration should be given to permitting workers to make use of the library during working hours. In time, this should become almost a neces- sity; for, as the worker becomes more professional, he will have to have—and come to expect—the same privileges normally accorded to professional-type employees. He may even have to be provided with financial help and assistance in purchasing appropriate books and journals as another possible way of encouraging him to keep current in his field of endeavor.

Some organizations are already active in this area of continuous training. One leading industrial company has developed mobile library units which operate on a regular schedule, visiting different parts of the plant and the various work groups at times when employee attention is most likely. In another case, current periodi- cals and recently published texts and books on the work subject, as well as areas of study which affect productivity, are wheeled onto the work floor on specially built carts, and workers are permitted to look over the material and encouraged to check it out.

Another way to attract interest is to have reprints made of signifi- cant and pertinent articles and give them to employees to whom the subject matter should be of concern. Or it may be feasible to develop a digest on a periodic basis which will consist of excerpts, condensations, and reviews of material which will help the employ- ees keep up to date and knowledgeable about future developments. Such a digest could be so edited and composed that it would trans- late into language suited to the average worker's level of literacy information that he might find difficult to follow in the original. Both the digest and reprints could be the take-off point for the regularly scheduled discussion sessions suggested earlier in this chapter.

A procedure for reviewing and selecting material for reprints and for the digest should be established in order to make certain that the information disseminated will accomplish the intended purpose and that the task will be handled systematically. Without system and firm guidelines, there will be the tendency to reprint simply for the purpose of reprinting—flooding the worker with information to the point where he will find it impossible to cope with and the project will achieve the status of being ridiculous. One likely solution is the establishment of a board composed of qualified personnel charged with the responsibility of selecting the material to be included. This body should of course be capable of discerning the applicability to the work process of the publications reviewed and so interpreting the information selected that it will be meaningful to the employees.

As in the case of the discussion meetings previously advocated, library resources and methods of encouraging reading should by no means restrict themselves to technical or work literature. Any area of study which will help employees gain a greater insight into the overall work environment and the nature of human conduct and response, as well as subjects which would stimulate greater interest in and attention to the work process, should be included in the library approach to continuous training, even though they might not normally be considered directly related to work activity.

Facilitating the Formation of Worker Associations

The organization of associations of knowledge workers as a vehicle for their development and progress should be encouraged. Associations are recognized media for transmitting new thought and methodology in most professions and in many occupations, and they should be able to serve the same purpose for the new breed of worker. The instruments man, parts programmer, electronics technician, or maintenance man will more and more find it necessary to get together with his colleagues in order to keep abreast of changes, just as is now the case with the scientific, medical, dental, engineering, or other professional man.

Such organizations are already evident among hospital employees at the technical level. Laboratory technicians, X-ray technicians, and even laundry supervisors have associations which very often meet on local, regional, and national bases, or they have the opportunity to attend special courses, conventions, or other gatherings to hear and discuss the latest developments in their specialty.

Profiting from Timely Training Opportunities

In addition, there are some special opportunities which should be taken advantage of as a means of affording workers exposure to advanced thought, predictions of future developments, and even anticipated near-term changes in their occupation. For example, the presence of visiting technicians and other scientific and engineering personnel could be an occasion to assemble those employees who work in the visitors' general area of specialization or a related field for lectures or discussions of current and advanced thinking, possible new concepts and their applicability, and the like.

Representatives of manufacturers of equipment and machinery used by the organization should be invited at planned intervals to gather with company employees who operate that equipment for the purpose of acquainting them with planned changes and innovations. Longer-term and futuristic-type developments that can be foreseen in equipment design and applicability, as well as worker qualifications necessary for effective operation, also can be introduced. Such sessions should enable the workers concerned to get answers to questions affecting their work and even to make suggestions for improvement.

Any type of breakthrough, even though it is only indirectly related to the worker and his work, can be an occasion for bringing employees together and informing them of its significance. This should not only help in broadening the employee's outlook but should also provide information which, although not directly related to his specific function, should develop in him an understanding of the total system and its purposes and, by so doing, result in better job performance. As an additional benefit, this kind of training demonstrates that the organization has respect for the employee and recognizes his new status and the importance of his function.

Consideration should be given to having workers undertake training at the installations of suppliers, on a systematically scheduled basis determined by the applicability of instruction, to fill long-term objectives. It is not necessarily immediate and noticeable results that should be the determining factor in reaching a decision on the advisability of this type of training; rather, management should consider its appropriateness in creating interest, stirring the imagination, and furnishing the kind of knowledge conducive to long-term proficiency and productivity.

A period of time—for example, two weeks—to be spent annually for purposes of instruction on the premises of a supplier whose products, expertise, and fundamental development ability contribute significantly to company success might be worthy of being included in training plans for selected employees. Although this would be costly, the benefits to be achieved make such a proposal deserving of serious attention. *Factory* cites the following advantages of vendor training to the student and the employer:

1. He [the student] is in a new and neutral environment—free of worries and pressures from home and boss.
2. He may see the break as an opportunity to kick bad work habits or attitudes.
3. He will likely be working with better facilities both for lectures and laboratory practice. Instructors are specialists in their technical field and in knowledge of how to train. Students have a chance to work on a wider variety of equipment without interruption and under conditions where observation is easy.
4. He is in an environment where he knows homework and out-of-class study is expected of him. You will probably get far more man-hours of his time per day than you could at home.
5. It is easier to train only the most promising men.
6. You are free from many of the labor problems and much of the haggling inevitable when training is offered at the plant. There's no free-loading by high-seniority, low-capability clock-watchers who insist on their right to attend classes.[7]

[7] Frank Hrabak, "Electronic Maintenance Training," *Factory* (now *Modern Manufacturing*), December 1962, pp. 64–65. Although referring specifically to electronics maintenance training, the cited benefits of vendor training are generally applicable.

This too is a major way of demonstrating employer concern about the status of employees and interest in their keeping up with changes in their occupations.

Vendor training can have an added benefit when representatives from other organizations are included in the makeup of the classes. This provides the opportunity of learning from others and their varied experiences, and it lends a semblance of prestige and professional status to the training sessions and their participants.

When vendor training is to be included in training plans, the following points should be taken into consideration:

1. Take time to talk with each man you choose for vendor training. Make sure he realizes his choice is actually a vote of confidence by the company in his ability and in his future. Most men will be anxious to exert the extra effort to merit the opportunity.
2. Ask your vendor what level of background training his course is directed to. Don't send men who can't keep up the required pace.
3. Be sure that your man knows what he is expected to accomplish at school and that your goals for him are realistic. Ask him beforehand if he is willing to do homework, study long hours, match wits with the best troubleshooters from other firms. Don't let him start the training until he knows exactly what types of the vendor's equipment are in the plant, and what kinds of trouble, if any, have been encountered with each.
4. Don't send a man and his supervisor to the same class if at all possible. They will probably both be reluctant to admit difficulties in understanding, to ask for special help, or to participate fully in group problem-solving. Each will be afraid that any comments or questions may reflect on his ability.
5. Make sure the vendor understands which men are to teach others when they return. These men need a somewhat different emphasis in their training, and far more background material.[8]

The present approach to training concentrates on teaching the

[8] *Ibid.*

worker his assigned task upon employment and on bringing him up to date, or attempting to retrain him, when his work changes or his skills become outmoded. This approach rests on the consensus that training efforts must be based on a real need, which implies that the need is sporadic. What must now be recognized is that in many industries and occupations the need is ever-present, and to consider training as a task to be performed only when dramatic changes in skill or job concepts take place means bearing the probable risk that the worker will not be mentally prepared to absorb new developments. Otherwise, considerable time and money will have to be spent on retraining, the success of which will be doubtful because worker knowledge and aptitude have not been kept up to date sufficiently to be able to profit from retraining.

Consider the engineer, the medical doctor, or the college professor who completed his formal education in 1960 and set aside very little of his time to keep up with changes in his work. It is easy to conclude that his professional proficiency has decreased considerably and that the task of bringing himself up to date, or being brought up to date, will be directly related to the time and effort which he has devoted to the almost day-to-day need for studying the developments taking place in his field of endeavor. If he has spent little time and effort on professional reading and studying, it will be most difficult—regardless of the length or intensity of refresher courses—to use such means as methods of updating his knowledge and techniques with a view to effective performance. His mind has simply not been kept alert; it is now too far afield from existing concepts to be able to grasp them properly.

Now consider the electronics technician, the instruments man, the engineer's assistant, or the automobile mechanic who completed his formal training in 1960. Unless he was given the opportunity to remain abreast of the new knowledge and new techniques which are continuously being developed, it will be very difficult now to retrain him, or bring him up to date, with periodic-type training programs.

In essence, the same requisites for continued effectiveness that exist in the professions are becoming increasingly prevalent at the worker level. However, this transformation of the worker's status and the nature of his work has not been generally accepted by the employer or the worker himself. This is significant; for, although it is expected that members of professions will utilize part of their time in studying and learning, this cannot as yet be realistically expected of the worker. The tendency is to surmise that continuous training is applicable only to the highly skilled; but, as Seymour L. Wolfbein concludes,

> The need for some continuous training component to match the needs generated by job and career changes over a lifetime is gaining substantial recognition. It is also being increasingly recognized that this training is needed by everyone, whether it is the surgeon specializing in mastoidectomies who becomes obsolesced by antibiotic procedures involving penicillin or the chemist faced with new photochemistry and radiochemistry; the skilled machinist who finds programmed numerical control able to deal with machine tools to the closest necessary tolerances or an unskilled highway hand who sees a piece of excavating equipment do the work of a dozen men.[9]

Until the time comes when the new breed of worker is accepted on more or less a professional basis, and until he looks at himself in this way, the employer will have to provide the opportunity, motivation, and tools for continuous training. Again, management must recognize and accept this basic change in order that the concept of continuous training may be put into effect and achieve the desired results.

---

[9] Seymour L. Wolfbein, *Education and Training for Full Employment* (New York, Columbia University Press, 1967), p. 58.

5

The Concept

of Total Training

TRAINING CAN NO LONGER BE SIMPLY TEACHING AND LEARNING, AND it involves much more than just attaining competence in a particular task or skill. It now requires that the direction of effort shift from job training to worker training. But even this change in emphasis will not satisfy the demands of the times. The day has arrived when training cannot be looked upon simply as an isolated aspect of productivity; rather, it must be viewed as an integral part of an overall plan to maintain and increase worker proficiency and contribution to the organization. The concept of training, therefore, as held and implemented in many organizations, must give way to the concept of development, or *total training*. The objective now becomes one of developing the worker in all areas and respects through which he can contribute to the organization. This necessitates giving attention to structuring the organization and insuring the type of supervision, as well as developing those worker traits, which will permit and encourage complete involvement and multi-faceted effectiveness.

Total training will require a realistic understanding of the new worker on the part of management and supervisory personnel, and the worker himself will have to look at his work and his situation in a different light. In addition to specific job or task effectiveness, the purpose of training becomes one of developing and preserving ability to adapt to change, breadth of knowledge, conceptual understanding, self-motivation, creativity and imagination, self-confidence, and independence in work—and of instilling in the employee an attitude of confidence and security which permits concentration on superior job performance. In the discussion of the need for introducing the worker to the job and to his environment, and in outlining the format for continuous training, emphasis was placed on developing these traits and enlarging their effectiveness and on looking at the worker from the standpoint of overall contribution. In essence, the whole process of training should have total training as its overriding objective, and this concept should be thought of not as being a separate phase of training but as playing a significant role in all parts of the process.

Independence and Self-Confidence

The new type of work and the modern-day employee make it necessary that our traditional assumptions about the worker and his work be reevaluated. Manual dexterity, which has been the principal ingredient in productivity, is yielding to mental ability. John Diebold states:

> Many of the new jobs that automation will create (supervising the intricate workings of delicate machines, for instance) will require an increasing ability to think and to judge, increased understanding of mathematical and logical methods, in short, increased education in the largest sense of the term. . . .

> Considerably fewer workers will be needed for routine monotonous jobs because machines will be doing that work. The jobs that will be reserved for people are those requiring judgment and those that a machine cannot readily be built to do—in other words, the more interesting ones.

The new jobs will call for less use of muscles and more use of judgment, since automatic machines are delicate and complex and call for a high level of skill and precision on the part of their human monitors.[1]

Most training philosophy and methodology are, however, geared to improving physical dexterity, as is evidenced by the insistence of training manuals and publications on the supervisor's teaching the job to the worker at the work station as though it were still mainly physical in nature. There is constant reference to the following four steps, often regarded as the gospel of training:

1. Put the worker at ease. Find out what he knows about the job, what fears he has, and how best to train him.
2. Show him how the work is to be done.
3. Have the employee do the work assigned while explaining verbally what he is doing.
4. Have the supervisor follow up to make certain that the correct procedure is being followed.

While it is true that there probably will always be some types of work (although they are steadily decreasing in numbers and importance) which will require this training approach, the characteristics of many of today's jobs do not lend themselves to these principles of training. How would you apply these four steps to an instruments man, a laboratory technician, an electronics specialist, a maintenance engineer, or the operator of the controls in an automated industry when each day may bring about an entirely different work problem? Or when, within one day, questions regarding procedure may demand varying answers and different methods of solution, requiring the worker to have good judgment and decision-making ability among other qualifications for effective performance?

In a discussion of worker qualifications required by automated processes based on their study of ". . . a changeover to automation in a baking company employing about 650 blue-collar workers . . . ," Professors Lipstreu and Reed state:

The machine monitors make adjustments as required by gauges, signals from bells, and routine quality control work conducted

<hr>

[1] *Beyond Automation* (New York, McGraw-Hill Book Company, 1964), pp. 148, 197.

at their work stations. But the degree of judgment required of these employees is definitely greater now because, though many of the decisions that must be made quickly are spelled out in job instruction manuals, and much of the decision-making function is consequently routine and well defined, the unexpected new problem looms constantly. Thus, each machine monitor must have considerably greater decision-making ability, even though he may need to call on this ability only intermittently. When it comes to machine technicians and maintenance personnel, of course, judgment skills are applied constantly.[2]

It is becoming increasingly apparent in many industries and occupations that a specific way of performing work is no longer applicable, nor can it be expected that the supervisor will always be present. Even if he could be on hand at all times when problems occur, it would be very difficult, as emphasized in a later section of this book on foreman training, for him to furnish specific solutions to the dissimilar technical problems which the work group under his supervision will encounter. The knowledge worker will have to handle his assignments on a more or less independent basis, which will require a much higher degree of self-confidence than is usually now encouraged in most occupations. The ideas expressed in Chapters 2, 3, and 4 will provide guidelines for increasing working independence and self-confidence, but these alone will not suffice unless complemented by the following training practices:

1. The worker should be allowed to determine, on his own, solutions to problems which arise in his work. The "learning by making mistakes" philosophy should, within reason, be adhered to. It is only in this way that the employee will gain the understanding of his work and the degree of independence and self-confidence required for him to be effective.
2. The novice should be assigned to work with an experi-

[2] Otis Lipstreu and Kenneth A. Reed, "Automation's Impact on Personnel Administration: A Case Study," *Personnel,* January-February 1965, p. 43. At another point in this article, in expressing their thoughts regarding qualifications for maintenance technicians, the authors conclude, "Specifications for these jobs must include broad, practical, engineering understanding, plus an almost uncanny ability to get a machine back in operation in minimal time," requiring "... training programs less broadly aimed than those of the typical college engineering curricula, but at a higher level and of a different nature than the typical trade course for machine mechanics." See pp. 44 and 46.

enced employee in the beginning in order that he may see and understand the practical application of the knowledge he has acquired in the classroom. This is not to advise an apprentice-type arrangement but, rather, to urge one in which the experienced worker acts somewhat like a consultant. And even at this point it is important that the "consultant" allow his protégé to be on his own as much as possible. He should not make decisions or do the work for him, but should see to it that the employee goes about making his decisions and performing his work in a logical and sensible way.

3. The supervisor and consultant must avoid the "mother hen" approach of constantly overseeing the work of the new employee, overprotecting him, and persistently correcting his thought processes and work procedures. If such an approach is really required, then the trainee is not qualified for the job.

4. In addition to being a counselor and adviser, the first-line supervisor must provide the encouragement, inspiration, and motivation which will help those in his charge to look upon their job assignment as being *their* work and give them the confidence to be more independent and self-confident. So different is this way of looking at the employee that the supervisor may not only have to aid him in assuming this role but also have to convince him that this is the desire of the organization.

These recommendations will not be as simple to put into practice as they first appear to be, for what is being advised is contrary to the accepted concept of the role of the supervisor. He must break away from this role, however, and—as explained in greater detail in another section of this book—become more of a consultant and administrator than a first-line supervisor in the conventional sense. In most cases, the trainee will probably be more anxious to become independent and self-confident in his work than the supervisor is willing or able to let him be, which indicates that time and effort may have to be devoted to training the supervisory level in this different view of their function.

Besides the almost absolute necessity, due to the changing nature of most jobs, that the worker become more independent and self-confident, there are other advantages to having him develop in this direction. Independence and self-confidence are symbols of trust, and a tangible way of recognizing the professional standing of the knowledge worker. Also, trust and recognition can be avenues for encouraging self-motivation and self-training, just as they can aid in activating the traits of creativity and imagination, all of which make for a more effective and loyal employee.

In their book *Industrial Jobs and the Worker,* Turner and Lawrence conclude, "Clearly, the more discretion that an operator can exercise concerning how to do his job, the less likely he is to be frequently absent from work."[3] What is significant in this statement is not so much the discipline of reporting for work as the indication that greater interest in the job is fostered when the worker can participate in determining the way in which his task is to be accomplished. This interest should result in better productivity and greater willingness on the part of the employee to contribute, not only to his job, but to the organization as well.

> Participatory management, say its proponents, will be the system of the future. This confidence is based on their analysis of the changing nature of the workforce. As automation takes over routine tasks of all sorts, they feel, the workforce eventually will fall, by and large, into two basic categories: those concerned with maintenance and those concerned with knowledge. Both groups, industrial psychologists assert, will do their best if self-motivated, rather than driven either by an authoritarian management or by an inexorably moving assembly line.[4]

The Worker's Sense of Security

Evidence is beginning to accumulate that absenteeism, job performance, accidents on and off the job, and emotional and mental stability are influenced by the worker's feelings regarding job security. Industrial physicians are now noting the growing signifi-

3 Arthur N. Turner and Paul R. Lawrence, *Industrial Jobs and the Worker* (Boston, Division of Research, Graduate School of Business Administration, Harvard University, 1965), p. 43.
4 "Can Employees 'Manage' Themselves?" *Dun's Review and Modern Industry,* November 1965, p. 60.

cance of emotional problems caused by urban living and by the new industrial environment, which tends to produce an attitude of uncertainty, fear, and inability to cope with contemporary job demands. They also point out that mental frustration, brought about by the realization that one's skills may be obsolescent, can seriously affect job performance in a negative way. Preoccupation about being unemployed, and possibly having to reduce one's standard of living, naturally makes it very difficult to concentrate fully on the job.

Not all mental stress, of course, is directly related to the new milieu, but it is estimated that 30 percent of the workforce has symptoms of mental or psychosomatic illness, or both, and that in 10 percent of these cases work performance is adversely affected. Part of the total direct cost of absenteeism, which amounts to $10 billion a year, can be attributed to psychological problems resulting from the pressures of insecurity due to workers' fear of technological obsolescence. Hence providing measures to help insure the emotional stability of workers becomes particularly significant in view of recent court decisions moving in the direction of holding the employer liable for workman's compensation to mentally ill workers.

What part can training play in building security and confidence in the worker and thus helping to insure the maximum possible employee effectiveness? The first requirement is the institution of a type of training program that will enable the employee to keep up with changes in his skill and occupation and help him to retain his employability. The second step is to inform the workers that the objective of company training policy is to insure their employability in this way. At the beginning of employment, the newcomer should not only be told how this is to be accomplished but should also be informed of the contribution he is expected to make to the program. Bear in mind, too, that training policy and plans must be well thought out, realistic, and convincing if the employee is to be sold on their applicability and believe that they provide for a greater degree of job security.

Building confidence in worker ability to keep up with change and in company ability to provide avenues for continuing employee effectiveness should be stressed. This can be done by citing examples of what the training program has already accomplished, how this was done, and what the qualifications of the training staff are. Pointing out specific workers who have been able to maintain their employability because of company training should be convincing evidence both of employee ability to cope with change and of the success of the company's training policy. In addition, citing the progress made by employees in other organizations in keeping up with change should serve to build confidence.

Worker security and confidence are not traits which are quickly developed, nor will they continue to prevail simply as the result of a one-time review of the steps just outlined. Company policy and success in training should be brought to the attention of the worker at sufficient intervals to insure understanding, belief, and accept-ance—so convincingly that the fears which prevent maximum con-tribution are minimized. Formal training sessions can be utilized for this purpose, but the task should also be one of the responsi-bilities of the immediate supervisor.

Conceptual View and Multiskills

The advisability of insuring, on the part of the employee, an understanding of the total work process of which his job is a part was urged in the section on introductory training. But the need for a conceptual view and understanding of work, and the growing demand for multiskilled workers, require that training give more emphasis to the development of both than is currently the case and that such development become an integral aspect of total training in addition to having an important role in introducing the worker to the job.

Modern-day work requires great interest, involvement, and loyalty to the task to be accomplished. One way to secure this interest, involvement, and loyalty is to make the worker feel that he is making a vital contribution to achieving the overall objective with which he is concerned. This requires that his importance, and the significance of his contribution, be recognized by management and that this attitude be transmitted to the employee. Giving the worker the opportunity of viewing his work from the standpoint of the total task to be accomplished, in addition to helping to make him proficient, will accomplish a great deal in the way of enabling him to better understand the nature and significance of his job and to become more deeply involved in it.

The efforts made in introductory training to help the employee grasp the relationship of his specific task to the total work process should be supplemented by additional practices. First, employees should be continuously apprised of the purpose and importance of their work: how it fits into the overall objective, what the reasoning is behind the determination of that objective, and its significance to company goals and plans. Simply going over this information during the introduction to the job is not sufficient, for it will tend to be subordinated to day-to-day performance and may be entirely forgotten. Securing worker involvement and interest, as well as fostering understanding and the conceptual point of view, requires constant promotion—as is the case with the successful achievement of any desired and continuing objective.

Any changes in company plans and purposes should be brought to the attention of the working force. This is particularly expedient when the change involves a significant aspect of the work or a specific work group. To insure effective comprehension, the change in plans or the new objective should be broken down to the point where it has meaning for the employees concerned in terms of the work to which they are assigned. Too often such a development is put into effect without transmission of its purpose, meaning, and requirements to those who are directly concerned. As a result, they are deprived of the awareness and knowledge necessary for competent implementation.

There is no doubt whatsoever that involvement, loyalty, and interest are adversely influenced by failure to convey the facts of impending change and the reasons for it to those who are to be subject to it. And the increasing frequency of change highlights the advisability of information sessions on change as an integral part of training. They are a prerequisite for that worker understanding which leads to effectiveness, and they provide the opportunity for employees to know and feel that they are an important part of the organization and are involved in its plans.

In their case study of Company X's changeover to automation, Lipstreu and Reed conclude, "*Automation necessitates training for psychological adjustments to change.*" They go on to describe how this was done:

> To prepare its employees for the move to the new plant, Company X discussed the change—albeit in a somewhat unsystematic

manner—through such devices as the house organ, new plant models, movies, letters, and plant tours. Individual interviews were held with all employees whose jobs or positions would be changed. Supervisors were briefed on developments at regular Saturday morning meetings and were urged to discuss various aspects of the move with their people.

... We were impressed by the initiative of one supervisor who held informal, voluntary discussion sessions at his home and at the plant during the new-plant construction period. The year-long orientation he conducted, with over 40 meetings, each at least three hours long, seems to have paid off. Of the 16 employees in his group, two have left the company for better jobs, but ten are effective, classified employees, and the other four are "bucking" for classified work. The participants in this autonomous indoctrination were enthusiastic about its helpfulness and their supervisor considers it his most significant training accomplishment.[5]

The authors add, "We are convinced that much more effort must be directed to company-sponsored, formalized programs for psychological adjustment of employees to a more automatic work environment. The finest technical training will lose much of its effectiveness without such orientation."[6]

The worker should not only be made to understand the total task of which he is a part—and its objective—but should also be acquainted with the various phases of work involved in completing the task in order that he may develop a multiskilled approach to his work. Providing him with a thorough grounding, as previously advocated, in the theory on which his job is based is one way of instilling an understanding of its relationship to the whole and thus furnishing the background necessary for multiskilled effectiveness.

Rotating employees in the various phases of the work should contribute to the development of multiskills. It should also broaden employee thinking considerably. With the merging of skills and the growing necessity for knowledge of several skills on the part of the individual employee, and with job proficiency requiring the ability to cover an even wider area of work, training for the conceptual point of view and multiskilled competence is becoming an economic necessity. And this kind of training, because of its broad base and

5 *Op. cit.,* p. 46.
6 *Ibid.*

multifarious approach, should do more than develop necessary know-how. It should increase the worker's mental and physical flexibility, and it should also free the individual from the traditionally narrow view of his work, thus enabling him to see the necessity for change, to retrain himself more readily, and to grow in creativity, judgment, and imagination.

Conceptual understanding should better enable the employee to make positive contributions to the organization, particularly when technological discoveries necessitate the replanning of work situations. That workers ought to be trained to make such contributions, that they should be permitted to use their initiative in this way, is intimated in the following statement:

> Some needed changes in process or product may inevitably threaten to decrease some of the high-scoring task attributes to which workers are responding favorably. If so, the most important thing to remember may be the importance, to these workers, of perceived autonomy. More clearly than in other situations, undesirable consequences of technological change can be avoided to the extent that these workers actively participate in recognizing the need for change and in planning its impact. They are likely, it would seem, to have both the predisposition and the ability to devise ways of adapting to needed change while preserving existing levels of commitment to the importance of the work itself and of total organizational goals.[7]

Goal Is Total Contribution

All training should be directed at developing and freeing the individual so as to encourage and permit him to make this optimum contribution to the organization, not only from the standpoint of a particular job assignment, but to the degree that he will willingly offer to the organization all the talents at his command and consider such behavior as part of his work. Although, at first glance, many may conclude that this goal is not realistic, to achieve it is probably one of the foremost desires of both the employer and the working force. That the goal exists and ranks so high in the hierarchy of human wants is evidence of its feasibility. The words *freeing* and *permitting* are used intentionally, for they are exactly what must

[7] Turner and Lawrence, *op. cit.*, pp. 124-125.

often happen first if the worker is to be provided with an environment conducive to developing the multitude of attributes and concepts which not only are desirable but are being increasingly demanded.

The remarks of Carl F. Stover, senior political scientist at Stanford Research Institute and director of Stanford University's Public Affairs Fellowship Program, commented before the Twentieth Annual ASTD Conference on the narrow way in which training is traditionally viewed and carried out. His remarks are both interesting and pertinent:

> It is difficult for me to talk about the "philosophy of training," because the ideas inherent in that philosophy, strictly construed, violate certain essential elements of my own philosophy. I am against training, because it involves the disciplining and conditioning of men to carry out certain functions in a prescribed way as part of a system, whether productive, organizational, or social. I am against it because it reflects a false view of man, because it involves the subordination of man to technique, and because, in the long run, it won't work. . . .
>
> Ultimately these efforts will fail, perhaps disastrously. First, they will fail because any function for which a man can be "trained" is also one for which a machine can be designed. In its ultimate perfection, the "Swiss watch" organization society will find man superfluous. Second, they will fail because man, no matter how well conditioned, will always have within him the seed of revolution against a system that makes him less than he is, or is capable of being. Ultimately, somewhere and somehow, that seed will flower. Meanwhile, the price of preventing its flowering will become an increasing burden on the energy of the whole. Third, they will fail because training men to be functionaries in a well-articulated system results in the loss of opportunities for the release of man's creative energies on which all societies, large and small, ultimately depend.[8]

The present view of work by employer and employee, and the resulting philosophy of expected conduct, supervision, and training, are not usually in tune with the attitude and outlook necessary for

[8] Carl F. Stover, "Observations on the Philosophy of Training." Reprinted by special permission from the August 1964 issue of *Training Directors Journal* (now *Training and Development Journal*). Copyright 1964 by the American Society for Training and Development.

the total-contribution concept. Consequently, the first step is the recognition of the necessity for a change in viewpoint about work and the worker. The second is the establishment of the environment which will make it possible to institute the training measures needed to bring about the desired worker and supervisory behavior and to develop the traits of worker independence, self-motivation, and imagination which are favorable to self-training.

The desire to accomplish, which is part of the makeup of the great majority of people, combines with ability to constitute the two principal human characteristics which lead to effectiveness. Ability can be improved by proper training, provided the trainees selected have the necessary qualifications. However, training which makes for ability will not alone insure total contribution. Nor will it establish the ambience which allows and promotes self-training and continued effectiveness. Much depends on instituting the kind of training aimed at establishing the relationships and milieu which will activate the inherent desire for accomplishment. This desire will remain dormant, or will fail to become fully active, if the approach to training is one which does not consider total contribution as a major objective. Self-training and self-motivation can be the greatest rewards of the training approach urged in these pages.

There is much evidence, in summary, to indicate that present-day training is far more applicable to the work of the 1930's than to that of the last half of the 20th century. This is a principal reason why disappointment with the results of training is so common and why top management frequently does not place much faith in its long-term benefits. Unless its overall objective is continuing total contribution by the worker, the most that can be expected is simply job performance in its narrowest concept, with the probability of worker obsolescence increasing with each day.

6

Organizing
for Accomplishment

UNTIL RATHER RECENT TIMES, NONHUMAN CAPITAL HAS BEEN USED
as the major criterion for judging productivity, and material
investment per worker has been long thought of as the principal
avenue for increasing output. To this day, many industrialists,
economists, labor leaders, and government spokesmen continue to
emphasize nonhuman capital as the major factor in productivity and
judge effectiveness almost solely in terms of return on such assets.
It is true that, in the past, the machine often controlled the human
element and the worker was subject to the physical assets with
which he worked; therefore, the availability and efficiency of physical assets were the major determinants of productivity. But, in an
increasing number of industries, the effectiveness of machinery and
equipment hinges on the decision-making ability and expertise of
the people who operate and maintain them.

The word "equipment" appears to be displacing "machinery" in current literature, implying that work and the status of the worker have undergone considerable change. Equipment connotes a tool for accomplishment which is secondary to human expertise, whereas machinery suggests dominance over the worker. No doubt the capital investment per worker will, in some cases, continue to be the major element of productivity, but in many areas it has already been supplanted by investment in human assets. This is a growing trend. In other words, the education, intelligence, and ability of the people in the organization weigh heavily in judging the capabilities of the enterprise. Also, it is increasingly recognized that this thinking is applicable to the worker as well as to management. Its relevancy is particularly striking when one considers that expansion plans are often thwarted by the nonavailability of technical and skilled personnel rather than by the scarcity of management talent.

It would be interesting to know the number of instances in which production quotas have been delayed, reduced, or abandoned altogether because of failure to take into consideration the availability of the knowledge worker or because the necessary training programs have been overlooked in planning for expansion or other accomplishment. In discussing the increasing significance of investment in human capital, a major bank states:

> With the massive growth of physical capital (plant and equipment, housing, inventories, etc.) together with the availability of voluminous statistics on capital assets and physical production, virtually all economic studies emphasized the role of nonhuman capital.

> But this one-sided view has led to some serious errors. Thus, it has been widely assumed that it is the increase in the amount of capital per worker that primarily explains the growth of productivity per worker in advanced economies. This belief has led to the use of simple capital-output ratios in planning for economic development of less developed countries, in which it was assumed that there was a fixed relationship between the amount of physical capital invested and the increase in output that could be expected. Results of such planning have often been quite disappointing in practice.[1]

[1] First National City Bank of New York in its August 1965 *Monthly Economic Letter.*

The statement goes on to point out the significance of the investment in human capital with respect to economic growth as revealed
in recent studies. It cites Edward F. Dennison's *The Source of
Economic Growth in the United States,* which concludes that 23
percent of the growth in real national income during the period
1929–1957 is due to the better-educated labor force, whereas the
increase in physical assets accounted for only 15 percent of the
growth during this time. The same trend has no doubt continued
since 1957 at an accelerated rate—which lends increased validity
to the supposition that the availability of competent human capital
will become more and more the major factor in the feasibility of
industrial growth and expansion and that efficiency and effectiveness
will be judged by the return on such capital rather than on the basis
of material assets.

Manpower planning and training have become important enough
to be cited by Harvard economist John T. Dunlop as being involved
in one of the five major forces shaping the U.S. economy and its
institutions. He describes this force as "the institutional changes
associated with continuing high employment which will involve
more—not fewer—headaches for managers" and characterizes its
"educational consequences" in the following words:

> A high employment economy requires a very much larger atten-
> tion to training of manpower primarily by management but also
> by organized labor and by government. It is not adequately
> recognized that business enterprises are in the educational busi-
> ness, training and developing the general and specific skills of a
> workforce. These activities apply to production and maintenance
> workers, clerical employees, as well as professional and mana-
> gerial groups. The reference here is not to financial support of
> education or payment for courses in educational institutions.
> Rather, the point is that a business enterprise is not merely pro-
> ducing goods and services; it is also in the business of developing
> and training the skills and capacities of its workforce. This edu-
> cation is a joint output with production.

He goes on to state:

> Obviously, a more broadly trained and versatile workforce facili-
> tates adjustments to technical and market changes as well as
> increasing the real security of the employee. A continuing high-
> employment economy is one in which enterprises spend signifi-

cantly more on training and manpower planning and development, and is also one in which these activities are more highly
related to the success of the enterprise.[2]

Impact on Organization Framework

What significance should this emerging concept of values have
for the organization? Is the present place of training in the organizational hierarchy one of sufficient status to cope with the emphasis
that must be placed on worker development in order to insure the
availability of competent human capital? Is the way in which the
organization presently looks at the training function compatible
with the role that it must play, not only to insure growth, but
simply to maintain an established position? How should the training
function be organized? How, if at all, should it participate in the
long-term planning of the enterprise and in its day-to-day operations? These are the types of questions that must be considered and
answered with reasonable surety so that the training function can
be adequately structured to serve the needs of the organization.

From Follower to Leader

In most organizations, training is considered to be a staff or
advisory function, and it is often not even permitted this humble
status. Rather than being called upon to consult with the line
organization regarding its role, it usually is relegated to the position
of having to respond to demands after the need has become
apparent. This need, which should have been predicted, generally
arises through failure to achieve stipulated goals for lack of human
capacity. There may have been no serious damage to the corporate

2 John T. Dunlop, "New Forces in the Economy," *Harvard Business Review,*
March-April 1968, pp. 123–124. He concludes this section of his article in words
which could well be looked upon as a major challenge to training: "For business
managers, the major consequences of continuing high employment are to be seen in
the enhanced role of long-range corporate planning, including (a) detailed manpower
projections, (b) much greater attention to training activities within and outside the
workplace as new and more disadvantaged sources of manpower are employed, and
(c) supervisory personnel policies required to make such recruits a productive workforce." See p. 125.

posture; for human skills, remember, have been viewed as secondary to physical capital. The acquisition, operation, and maintenance of plant and machinery have always played a much more important role in corporate affairs than did a highly educated, knowledgeable workforce. It has seemed a rather simple task to train employees for the modest (and what would now be defined as elementary and unsophisticated) skills that formerly were needed to achieve the expected productivity. But the situation is now reversed: It is much easier to acquire plant and equipment than it is to obtain qualified personnel to operate and maintain these physical assets.

Money and the placing of an order will usually, within a reasonable time period, provide the desired material resources, but the availability of the knowledge worker requires long-range planning and the implementation of that planning with applicable day-to-day procedures. Although this is becoming more readily apparent, the organization has not, in most cases, been structured to provide the necessary framework for insuring that proper attention is given to this changed hierarchy of corporate values. The competence of any organization which, 10 or 20 years ago, laid out plans for expansion without considering its needs for physical capital would have been seriously questioned by the business community. Yet, today, plans are being made which fail to attach sufficient importance to manpower needs, much less develop means of finding and retaining the type and number of personnel needed. And very little is being accomplished in the way of providing the contemporary worker with the help and direction required to insure his continuing effectiveness.

To satisfy the demands of the times and to give cognizance to the new concept of corporate values requires that the following points be given serious consideration, keeping in mind the objective of structuring the organization in such a way that training will assume more of a leadership status:

■ The development of the human assets of the enterprise should be given a more important role in the organization. In some cases it may be advisable to shift training from a staff to a line function, and in other situations it may even be prudent to place it on the same authority level as the chief operating executives.

■ In decision making, greater weight and some degree of precedence should be given to the process of training, particularly the concepts of continuous and total training. The precedence accorded training should be determined by the importance of the knowledge-type worker to the future of the organization and its objectives. In those industries where progress requires an adept, intelligent employee, able to modify his aptitudes and possibly even change skills to meet differing demands, it may be necessary to give training goals more emphasis than immediate production goals. This may result in slower financial returns, but it is the only way to insure long-term economic success.

■ In the planning function, the continuous development of the workforce should be deemed as important as the acquisition and maintenance of capital equipment—if not more so. It is particularly logical that this be the case where human skills are more meaningful to success than physical capital.

■ Personnel should be made more training-conscious. This can be accomplished by training-emphasis programs using a strategy similar to that which is utilized to make employees safety-conscious. Very few of us would deny that having a workforce recognize the significance of training is at least as important as having employees realize the advisability of always thinking in terms of safety. Yet programs aimed at increasing training-consciousness are almost unheard of.

Coupled with programs to promote the recognition of training as a part of work is the necessity of conditioning the organization and its employees to accept and make use of the new ways of doing things and the other benefits which should accrue from training. It is too often the case that training ends in wasted time and effort and results in no return on funds expended, not because the training has been unsuccessful, but because of the unwillingness of the organization to recognize its value and permit the application of what could be positive and effective results.

However well an individual has learned a useful skill, that in itself by no means guarantees action. Bitter experience in plenty ought to have taught us that. A participant returning from training often finds his new capacities ignored, even resented. He looks for support, finds instead indifference or opposition. Doubts assail him about the usefulness of his training. His enthusiasm wanes. Soon he accepts his colleague's advice to "forget it." And so another man has been trained only into disappointment and frustration. Next time he will know better than to invest so much of himself in new initiatives and developments.[3]

Acceptance of the usefulness of training must be part of the thinking and behavior of management and must be transmitted through the echelons of the organization if it is to be expected that supervisory personnel and other workers—the human side of the workplace itself—will consent to let fellow workers put into effect what they have learned. "Without commitment to change at the top, the organization as a whole cannot move in the direction of innovation even though there may be islands of innovations, subunits of the organization, moving toward innovation to the extent that they can."[4]

Giving the training function a place of greater significance and stature in the organization should indicate to employees that the development of human attributes is not only a prime objective of the organization but also a sign that innovation resulting from training is welcomed and encouraged. The best approach, in many cases, will be to select for appointment or promotion to high position those executives who have demonstrated a sincere interest in training, who have some background in the function, or who have shown that they recognize the importance of training. This is particularly desirable in the areas of production and research and development, for the success of these divisions in many industries will depend to a great degree on the significance given to training. Staffing positions with training-oriented executives should contribute more to the accomplishment of long-term objectives than

3 Rolf P. Lynton and Udai Pareek, *Training for Development* (Homewood, Ill., Richard D. Irwin, Inc., and the Dorsey Press, 1967), p. 8. Reprinted by permission.

4 Donald A. Schon, *Technology and Change* (New York, Delacorte Press, 1967), p. 125.

appointing personnel who place major emphasis on the achievement of immediate and short-term goals.

Day-to-Day Makeshifts or Planned Development

One of the major reasons for the difficulty presently being encountered in keeping the workforce abreast of new developments results from lack of long-term planning in the area of training. Training departments are not usually given the responsibility of preparing employees on a long-term basis; and, even when this may be the case, they often lack the authority to enforce any plan which they may consider advisable. Those who are in line positions are so inherently concerned with day-to-day effectiveness that they have very little time or incentive to occupy themselves with other than immediate problems. The result is that no one in the organization has either the inclination or the duty to think out and put into effect training plans based on intermediate and long-term objectives.

Most often, employees are found to be lacking in ability, and the training department is then called upon to organize and conduct courses designed to remedy specific work deficiencies. These courses are of necessity constructed hurriedly, and they are aimed mainly at minimizing the particular area of trouble. Because of the immediate nature of such programs and their singleness of purpose, the results are usually not as good as they could have been; and not very much is really accomplished in solving the basic employee weaknesses in skill or work theory which brought about the necessity for specific courses in the first place.

What is called for is a change of thinking and a more direct effort to bring training plans in line with present and future requirements. Thus:

1. Responsibility and authority for training must be delineated. More, its role must be defined and strengthened in order that its objectives and purposes may be in accord with the needs of the organization and its functions clearly understood. The steps outlined under the heading "From Follower to Leader" will accomplish a great deal in the direction of making this a reality.

2. The long-term plans of the organization should be broken down to the point where their effect on training can be determined. The objective is to arrive at a type of training program which will insure the existence of a workforce readily able to adapt to changing demands and implement the established plans. This requires the following kind of analysis:

   ▪ What are the plans for the future?

   ▪ What worker qualifications will these plans require, and how many of what types of employees will be needed?

   ▪ What is the ability and knowledge status of the existing workforce in relation to future requirements?

   ▪ What kind of plans will be required to provide the employees with the desired knowledge and skills so that they can readily adapt to new demands with minimum retraining and hurried, single-purpose courses can be avoided?

3. The findings of this kind of analysis should be used to develop training plans in keeping with the concepts of continuous and total training.

Scheduled, Not Sporadic, Training

A regular schedule, to be followed by the employees concerned, should be devised in order to implement training plans. This schedule should have as its objective the provision of a practical way for employees to keep not only abreast but ahead of the knowledge requirements in their work area and, by so doing, insure the availability of a qualified workforce for present and future demands. Implied here is a dramatic shift away from the training philosophy that concerns itself purely with the conducting of courses after the need arises. We have already mentioned the wide acceptance, in industry, of safety training, which is performed on a more or less continuous basis and has as its objective the prevention of accidents. What is now recommended is the adoption of this same kind of approach for skill and knowledge training; in other words, the development and following of a continuous-type schedule which will decrease the likelihood of employee obsolescence and reduce or eliminate the necessity for retraining programs. It is strange that organizations should place so much emphasis on safety indoctrination, and so little on skill and knowledge development, when the latter is much more meaningful to success. Perhaps it is because safety is the only aspect of training which the organization permits the training department to perform; therefore, the group often becomes the *safety department*.

The idea of scheduled and continuous training as part of the workweek is indeed out of the realm of current practice. But if industry finds it to be prudent to establish and rigorously adhere to a maintenance schedule for machinery and equipment, which has as its purpose keeping these assets in condition so as to make continuous operation possible and increase long-term efficiency and effectiveness, it seems reasonable to conclude that this same practice should prevail in the case of the organization's human assets. With the predominant role being played by the knowledge worker, it is of growing importance to the intermediate and long-term success of the enterprise that a maintenance schedule for human capital be devised and enforced.

This schedule is absolutely essential to the classroom and the group approach, which should replace the old apprentice methods of training. Worker training is, in fact, now going through the type of transition that has occurred in preparing people for other types of occupations. At one time, practically all learning was conducted on an apprentice basis, but the nature of the work and the surrounding conditions changed to such a degree that apprenticeship was no longer feasible. Medicine and law moved from learning on the job to the classroom. Engineering schools evolved because of the increased significance of technology and also because industry could not develop engineers by the apprentice method as it had developed others before them.

The same process is now occurring in the case of hospital technicians, who once learned their skills on the job. But, as more knowledge than skill came to be required, special schools were started for training hospital personnel, and now colleges are introducing various types of curricula to educate laboratory analysts,

X-ray technicians, and other specialists. Nursing education as well is moving from the hospitals, where training was conducted principally by apprenticeship methods, to the colleges and universities. One of the major reasons for this change is the necessity for a background in theory and basic education in order to cope effectively with the analyses required for decision making in modern-day nursing and to provide the mental framework for understanding change.

> The knowledge needed by the nurse practitioner today differs greatly from that needed 20 or even 10 years ago. She is now being required to master a complex, growing body of knowledge and to make critical, independent judgments about patients and their care.
>
> It is recognition of this need for mastery of a complex body of knowledge, and the continuing need to learn and improve practice, that has led the association to believe that: *The education for all those who are licensed to practice nursing should take place in institutions of higher education....*
>
> Such practice requires knowledge and skill of high order, theory-oriented rather than technique-oriented. It requires education which can only be obtained through a rigorous course of study in colleges and universities.[5]

Not only is a more formal approach to occupational preparation developing in all these areas, but we are also witnessing a return to the classroom on a regularly scheduled basis by those employed in these occupations, in order that they may obtain the new knowledge required for maintaining job effectiveness.

This does not mean that college preparation is a basic requirement in qualifying for modern-day jobs, although many junior and community-type colleges are stressing curricula directed at developing the knowledge worker and many companies find it advantageous to recruit their workers from candidates who have had at least a year or two of college education. What is being emphasized is that the concept of work in industry is evolving at so rapid a rate, as is the case with many other occupations, that training must be more professional.

[5] "American Nurses Association First Position on Education for Nursing," *American Journal of Nursing*, December 1965, p. 107.

Foreman Status and Training

The role which the foreman or first-line supervisor performs should provide the basis for determining the training which he should receive and his place in the training function. It is not unusual to observe situations where the opposite approach predominates. That is, certain assumptions are made regarding the status of the first-line supervisor without first making an effort to determine his actual position and the responsibilities he can most effectively assume in maximizing performance and productivity.

The supervisor's job is often defined as consisting of providing on-the-job training, supervising the work, coordinating performance, maintaining high morale, motivating personnel, and being the principal link between management and the worker. That he can handle all these duties satisfactorily is questionable; indeed, there is considerable evidence to indicate that his role can no longer be what classical management theory held it to be. In all probability, at least some of the problems of inadequate worker productivity and undesirable employee-employer relationships result from the foreman's trying to function as called for by theory or company policy.

For example, it has already been brought out that the traditional practice of having the foreman act as the principal trainer at the work station is not applicable to modern-type jobs. As was stated, the first-line supervisor can act in such a capacity when the work is of a repetitive, apprentice-type nature, requiring more physical dexterity than mental aptitude. However, when flexibility, basic knowledge, mental ability, and skill at analysis and decision making become the principal attributes of worker effectiveness, it becomes obvious that the first-line supervisor can no longer be relied upon to assume the major responsibility for training.

The fact that the foreman or supervisor is expected to perform a training role is revealed by field research to be one of the chief stumbling blocks in the way of the adoption and implementation of modern training methodology. Both training and line personnel —in fact, the whole organization—are still very much oriented to the concept of the foreman as the principal trainer. As a result, he frequently gets the blame for failing in a duty which he is no longer able to handle. Training personnel point accusingly at the first-line supervisor as the weakest link in achieving their objectives, and they complain continuously about the lack of training ability at the foreman level, citing this as a major reason for their difficulty in coping with the problem of keeping the workforce up to date.

What must be recognized is that the nature of work in many industries is no longer of the type which lends itself to such reliance on the foreman level as a major medium for effective training. In industries where this is the case, courses designed to teach training methodology to foremen are of very little value and may even have a negative effect. They give the foreman the sense of an obligation which he cannot really fulfill; thus they result in considerable frustration on his part and lead the worker to question management's competence when the foreman attempts to train him in the conventional manner.

Nor can we expect the foreman to *supervise* his workers in the traditional sense of the term; for the work, in an increasing number of industries, is not the kind that is subject to supervision from the traditional point of view. Because, as previously discussed, much of modern work depends on individual decision making and accomplishment rather than on assembly-line productivity, the tasks for whose performance the supervisor is responsible are so varied that he cannot possibly have a sufficient grasp of all of them to oversee them from a technical standpoint. That is why the first-line supervisor is really becoming an administrator or group leader, distributing the assigned work, evaluating the judgment (not the work itself) of the employees subject to his surveillance, and helping to create and maintain a type of environment which is conducive to productivity. Peter Drucker says we must recognize that:

> ... This new worker cannot be supervised and that his performance cannot be easily measured. He can only be motivated. He must reach for excellence. He must want to contribute. He must try to develop himself, his capacity, and his contribution. All we can do is pay him. The supervision that we could give to the manual worker simply cannot be applied effectively to people who have to contribute their knowledge, conceptual skill, imagination and judgment.[6]

6 Peter F. Drucker, "Managing the Educated," *Management's Mission in a New Society*, edited by Dan H. Fenn, Jr. (New York, McGraw-Hill Book Company, 1959), p. 172.

Implications for Supervisory Training

Although the function of the first-line supervisor is changing, this does not preclude the advisability of training him in certain fundamental areas which will probably continue to be part of his job or seeking to improve his effectiveness. Indications are that foreman training, particularly as it concerns new appointees to the job, is often lacking in basic concepts. Bradford B. Boyd, in his research on the problems of transition from worker to supervisor, concludes that the following points should be given greater emphasis in foreman training in order to provide for better performance:

- The first job seems to be to recognize the needs of the supervisor just entering management's ranks. He should be told what the job is and why he was selected to fill it. He needs to know how he and his department relate to staff functions and other departments. He needs to feel he belongs to management. He is enthusiastic and has faith in his management. This enthusiasm should be nurtured and frequently rekindled. . . .

- Much wider use of presupervisory training programs is indicated covering management philosophy, management responsibilities of the foreman, introduction to the formal organization, and the union contract. Where size of the firm does not warrant such a program, a well-organized break-in period under a successful foreman is most desirable to realize the new man's potential more quickly.

- Establish well-defined avenues of communication to stimulate "talking things over." Coaching in the early months of supervision with frequent, informal performance review seems essential.

- Define standards of performance which the supervisor can use to appraise his own performance and progress. He will then know the criteria upon which his superiors are basing their evaluations of his performance. Particularly helpful to understanding "how am I doing" are standards based upon results expected.[7]

[7] Bradford B. Boyd, "Worker to Supervisor—Problems of Transition," *Personnel Journal*, September 1964, p. 426.

In light of the changing concept of responsibility, foreman training should stress those factors which provide the basis for effective administration rather than traditional supervision. For instance, one of his principal roles is to be thoroughly familiar with company policy, spirit, and outlook in order to keep employees properly informed and to be a responsive source of facts and data that are of interest to the worker. Therefore, the training of the foreman should have as one of its major objectives that of keeping him informed of all matters which might concern the employees. This should go further than simply apprising him of worker benefits, company rules, and similar matters; it should include expanding his knowledge of company plans and expectations, promotion possibilities, company interest in the worker, and other information which can aid him in fostering among the rank and file greater involvement in the work of the organization. (One example of this kind of training is the program shown in the schedule on pages 108–109.)

Caution should be exercised to prevent the subject matter from being simply factual in nature. It should, to be really effective, give evidence of company concern, interest, and commitment to the employee and to the desire that he become an integral part of the organization. It should include the type of information which, when passed on to the worker, will help him to feel that management is giving him consideration, opportunity, and recognition as being important enough to be kept advised of company plans, objectives, and prospects.[8] As a result, the organization should receive from the employee a greater degree of dedication, involvement, and sense of responsibility.

Another principal aim of foreman development is to provide an understanding of worker attitudes and behavior. Rensis Likert states that "supervisors with the best record of performance focus their primary attention on the human aspects of their subordinates' problems and on endeavoring to build effective work groups with high performance goals."[9] Also to be considered is the fact that since the performance of the knowledge worker depends more on his attitude, outlook, and motivation than was the case with his prede-

[8] For an interesting procedure for training in labor relations see Arthur F. Strohmer, Jr., "Labor Relations Training for Foremen: A New Approach," *Personnel Journal*, January 1968, pp. 48, 49, 55.

[9] Rensis Likert, *New Patterns of Management* (New York, McGraw-Hill Book Company, 1961), p. 7.

PRE-SUPERVISORY TRAINING

ALUMINUM COMPANY OF CANADA LTD. Arvida Works

Program Schedule and Content of Training

Responsible Department or Service: Activity	Time Spent	Objectives
		TRAINEES WILL:
Training: Introduction and Course Orientation	½ day	Feel at ease in new situation; get to know program directors; become aware of program objectives, content, schedules, and physical arrangements.
Training and other appropriate functional groups: Modern Supervision	1 hour daily, plus 8 half days	Understand basic principles of modern supervision (planning, organizing, controlling, etc.) and be able to use simple techniques of supervision in their daily work.
Visits: General Plant, Power House, Port, Research and Development, Plant Effluents Control, Public Relations, Traffic	10 half days	Have an overview of the Company's complete operation; have better appreciation of role of their units in the whole; appreciate how Company meets customer requirements and fulfills its role as a member of the community.
Plant Manager	½ day	Know the Plant Manager as a person and appreciate some wider problems of running the business.
Communications: The Company	3 days	Know something of the Company's structure, major activities, and markets; be aware of some problems of communications and of the help available; be familiar with some of the Company's communications media.
Employment	3 days	Know and understand Company employment policies and practices for bargaining unit employees; understand their role in making policies effective; be able to answer employees' questions.
Payroll	1½ days	Be able to prepare documents necessary to insure employees are correctly paid; know pay procedures; be able to answer employees' questions.
Employee Benefits	2 days	Know and understand important aspects of employee benefit plans; be able to answer easy questions on these; understand how these plans apply to themselves.

Note: Prepared by Dorothy Pertuiset and reprinted with her permission.

Responsible Department or Service: Activity	Time Spent	Objectives
Industrial Engineering	8 days	Become acquainted with techniques of work measurement, time studies, determining rest periods, work sampling, job evaluation plan; understand how industrial engineering can help them as supervisors.
Safety and Medical	3 days	Understand roles of safety department and of supervision in maintaining employee safety and health; know what to do in case of accident; know how to make medical services useful to employees; be able to give artificial respiration and heart massage.
Fire Prevention	½ day	Be able to collaborate effectively in prevention and control of fire hazards.
Mechanical Maintenance	½ day	Be able to appreciate financial advantages of effective maintenance and understand how supervisors can help reduce maintenance costs.
Electrical Power Electrical Maintenance Instrument Maintenance	1½ days	Understand key role of power in plant operation; know how to make best use of maintenance services.
Purchasing	½ day	Be able to prepare purchase orders correctly; know how to use warehouse services.
Employee Relations	5 days	Be able to administer sections of collective labor agreement relevant to supervisors; be able to participate in processing employee grievances; know how to get help in interpreting agreement; know how employees can use counseling services.
Training: Employee Appraisal	1 day	Be able to make performance appraisals; understand ways to help improve employee performance.
Training: Job Instruction	3½ days	Be able to prepare a simple job instruction program and teach to employees.
Course Evaluation	½ hour at end of each activity; ½ day at end of a program	Program monitors and directors will be able to determine how well they have met trainees' needs and modify future programs accordingly.

cessor when machinery helped set the pace of productivity, it follows that the worker must be given more attention than the work itself. Even in those cases where jobs are repetitive in nature and machine-controlled, an understanding of worker status and outlook can play a significant part in instilling the desire to excel. A recent study, although claiming to be preliminary rather than definitive, states:

> ... There is little doubt that when the technology requires repetitive and intrinsically dissatisfying work, the foreman who understands his workers' attitudes, who listens to what they like and dislike about the job, and who encourages job rotation and informal ways of increasing job involvement can to a significant extent counteract the negative impact of the technology.[10]

Not to be overlooked is that the objectives and success of several aspects of total training brought out in Chapter 5 depend on the first-line supervisor's having a good knowledge of job and behavioral situations and their effect on worker response and vice versa.

The Supervisor's Growing Dilemma

Interviews with management reveal the growing dilemma of the first-line supervisor and point to the increased advisability of training which promotes an understanding of the knowledge worker, his sense of values, and the way he looks at things. Management frequently laments the difficulty foremen are having in communicating with the workers in their charge, very often resulting in worker resignation or loss of respect for the first-line of supervision. Instances of employees sneering or laughing at the foreman behind his back appear to be on the increase.

A typical case will show what is often taking place. The owner of a contracting firm, a college graduate, reported that he was having a problem retaining young employees at the worker level. He admitted that they were smarter, more intelligent, and quicker

[10] Arthur N. Turner and Paul R. Lawrence, *Industrial Jobs and the Worker* (Boston, Division of Research, Graduate School of Business Administration, Harvard University, 1965), p. 117.

to learn their jobs than those workers he had hired ten years earlier, but they did not seem to have as much interest in their work and became dissatisfied soon after employment. The result was increased employee turnover. The owner found, however, that he could talk to these young workers sensibly about the tasks to be accomplished more than had been the case with prior groups. Also, they seemed to be quite content with their work when he was supervising them.

The conclusion was reached, after analyzing and studying the situation, that the foremen and the young workers under their supervision came from two different schools. The foremen, from the old school, had only a seventh-grade or junior-high education; they had grown up in a more staid and conservative environment. They followed the rules of close supervision (which was the way *they* were bossed) and permitted no deviation from established work methods. The newer employees were almost all high-school graduates brought up in a more permissive society; they had developed a degree of independence, disliked being told what to do, and wanted a type of satisfaction from their work that close supervision would not permit. And the work itself also had changed, requiring more autonomy and decision making at the worker level.

The workers and their foremen thus spoke two different languages and had different outlooks and value systems, which made understanding, communication, and compatibility almost impossible. Each group saw the work to be done in a different light and from a different point of view. In essence, the two represented dissimilar cultures. The situation, if not recognized and given consideration in job definition and supervisory methods, could only lead to conflict and dissatisfaction. The work and the workers both having changed, the latter were no longer willing to be bossed in the old way.

Management had overlooked training the foremen so as to develop in them the perspective and the way of doing things necessary to cope with changing worker outlook, education, status, and response. Nor had management provided the kind of program which would enable first-line supervisors to grasp changing work and behavioral concepts. What was missing was a continuous reevaluation of the supervisors' approach and methods and their understanding of the need for allowing—and, in fact, encouraging—

greater independence in job performance and a broader view of the work by the young employees.

More Revolutionary than Evolutionary

The training of foremen in worker attitudes and behavior should be continuous, for attitudes and behavior are evolving constantly and, to some, the nature of the change is more revolutionary than evolutionary. What should be recognized is that the changing work situation demands not only training the worker in the technical and scientific aspects of the work, but also impressing on the supervisory staff the magnitude of the impact of change on worker behavior and attitudes. Only in this way can the supervisor fulfill his administrative and consultative responsibilities effectively.

Let us say it once again: Not only the *work* but the *worker* is affected by rapid advances in technology. With each new generation—possibly every ten years—people are brought up in a different culture, with an outlook and values that are different from those of their seniors. They must therefore be viewed and supervised accordingly if maximum worker contribution and commitment are to be achieved. The point being stressed is that supervisors should undergo continuous training to acquaint them with the effects of changing culture and environment on their subordinates. This will enable them to adopt methods of dealing with the workers in their charge which are compatible with their own makeup and conducive to insuring the desired response.

The need for new concepts of supervision and administration to meet changing behavior is also becoming recognized at the executive level.

> Increasingly, top managements in some of the best-run companies are beginning to note that the old motivational tools are losing their edge. Yet only a few suspect the reason: Slowly and subtly, as a new generation of talent takes over at middle and top management levels, a new motivational value system is evolving among executives. In fact, the pattern of motivational priorities is being reshuffled.[11]

[11] Arch Patton, "Executive Motivation—How It Is Changing," *Management Review,* January 1968, p. 4.

Supervisory training should obviously concern itself with developing the judgment of supervisors, so that they can determine whether or not work is being performed according to plans and expectations and effectively evaluate the decisions of employees regarding their work. This involves more than an understanding of the technical aspects of the tasks under their supervision. It requires a good knowledge of basic theory and also a comprehension of the total concept of the work to be accomplished; for the supervisor really becomes more of a consultant to workers regarding their work, and the way it is best done, rather than a director of performance.

Training should further give emphasis to the process of evaluating problem areas, determining alternatives, and making decisions so that the foreman can determine whether or not the workers have followed the best procedure in arriving at solutions to diverse and complex situations. In other words, as the knowledge worker becomes chiefly concerned with work requiring more mental aptitude than manual dexterity, the supervisor must become an adviser, overseer, and judge of thought processes for those under his surveillance rather than a foreman of the work itself. It follows, then, as with worker training and supervisory training in the area of behavior and attitudes, that judgment training also must be of the continuous type. It should not take the form of just a two- or three-week course in decision making, but should consist of regularly scheduled lectures and discussions held at reasonable intervals to acquaint the supervisors with expected developments in the work process, trends in the evolution of work, long-range forecasts of the impact of technology on job definition and performance, and changes taking place in the basic thought on which the work is based.

Unions and Training: Reaching an Accord

The willingness of the union to cooperate with the employer in implementing training philosophy and procedures which are germane to a particular job situation will depend to a great extent on the attitudes and the spirit of trust and confidence which have been established through prior relationships by the parties concerned.

Where there is mutual respect and an air of faith in one another prevails, and where sensible efforts have been made to insure that the nature of the training problem is understood and accepted, very little difficulty should be encountered in reaching a satisfactory agreement.

When resistance or hostility is met with, it is probably due not so much to the proposed program as to behavior patterns developed from past experience. Negative reaction may also stem from management's failure to explain the problem and circumstances in such a way as to invite favorable reception, or the proposed method of implementation may make it hard for the union or its leaders to permit themselves to be cooperative. What must be recognized is the naturally intense motivation on the part of union members and their officers to maintain their strength and security. Consequently, any change in training philosophy must incorporate measures which will assure the continuance of union status and the confidence of its members, as well as alleviate possible economic fears and mental reservations as to the effect of training on job standing.

A stalemate is often reached over the question of who is going to get credit for a new approach to training. Sometimes the situation is such that the objectives of continuing proficiency and resulting productivity on the part of the organization are forgotten. Yet credit is far and away secondary to acceptance and implementation. It should be expected that to maintain the respect of their members and, in fact, insure their own job security, union officers will think it important that they be cited as being responsible in whole or in part for training innovations that depend on their approval for success. It is better to accede to their demands than to insist stubbornly that credit redound to the employer on the basis that it is his money, time, and ideas which are at stake. Such adamance is only too likely to result in failure to secure union cooperation and a workforce that will gradually lose its ability to insure the company's competitive position.

If past relationships have not been favorable, a more studied approach, taking into consideration the sensitivities involved, is applicable. Under such circumstances it is particularly advisable that, in the planning stages, the reaction of the union be anticipated and given sincere attention. Any type of negotiation between two or more parties with agreement as the goal should be preceded by sincere efforts to understand the way the different groups will probably view the proposal in question. But it is even more important that such a procedure be followed when discord rather than harmony has been the rule.

An objective analysis of the union position relative to the concepts requiring agreement should be undertaken by management before submission to the employee representatives. The union's possible points of view should be studied and should affect the way the training need is to be handled, how it is to be presented, and how it is to be implemented. An understanding of the union attitude toward training and the reasoning and circumstances which have contributed to the members' thinking on the subject can aid considerably in shaping training proposals that are more likely to be accepted and in adopting a procedure for negotiations that will be successful.

Training and management personnel alike may be tempted not to adopt new training philosophies and methods on the assumption that the union will not agree to them and, therefore, any positive effort to institute changes is hardly worthwhile. Field research reveals that it is not unusual for training-department representatives to cast blame on the union, with its supposedly negative attitude, as the major obstacle to effective results—only to discover that the union has never been approached. And the literature on the subject indicates a recognition by union officials and members of the need for a different approach to training.

> . . . It must not be forgotten that we are living in a time of rapid technological change that will require great flexibility and adaptability of workers in many of the skilled trades. The substitution of quickly trained, narrow specialists for rounded craftsmen could prove exceedingly costly in the long run. At the very least, it would certainly limit the mobility of the individuals affected.[12]

Moreover, ". . . Local 1 of the International Brotherhood of Electrical Workers, in St. Louis, in cooperation with the Federal Office of Apprentice Training and a local vocational school, has set up what it calls a 'postgraduate school' for training in new electrical tech-

---

[12] Nat Weinberg, in *Toward a Manpower Policy*, edited by Robert Aaron Gordon (New York, John Wiley & Sons, Inc., 1967), p. 344.

niques. Within a short time, 400 members signed up for a three-year course and were attending 38 different classes four nights a week."[13]

In numerous cases where management takes the attitude that the union will surely be obstructive, the members and their leaders may, on the contrary, recognize the need for a new approach to training and be willing to cooperate in its planning and implementation. They have simply felt that management should be the first to show interest by taking the initiative. Blaming the union or anyone else may indicate complacency, ineffectiveness, or lack of ability to handle training by those responsible.

Unions and Training: The Future

There is much to indicate that the strength and perhaps the survival of labor unions as they exist today will depend at least in part on the attitude, outlook, and willingness to cooperate which they develop regarding the education and training of their members.

To repeat: Employability will more and more be determined by the avenues available and by the encouragement and incentives provided to facilitate keeping abreast of changes in occupations. Job security and the status and treatment accorded the worker by the employer will rest on the continuing adeptness and competence of the employee; they will be less and less determined by membership in an organized power structure. It is already apparent in the adverse trend shown by union membership that further progress in organizing workers will be increasingly difficult unless the unions' thinking and the direction of their efforts recognize other objectives. To state the matter simply, many of the needs which unions once served no longer exist or are not as significant as they once were. John K. Galbraith, writing on union status in his provocative book *The New Industrial State,* puts it this way:

> The industrial system, it seems clear, is unfavorable to the union. Power passes to the technostructure and this lessens the conflict of interest between employer and employee which gave the union much of its reason for existence. Capital and technology allow

[13] John Diebold, *Beyond Automation* (New York, McGraw-Hill Book Company, 1964), p. 145.

the firm to substitute white-collar workers and machines that cannot be organized for blue-collar workers that can. The regulation of aggregate demand, the resulting high level of employment together with the general increase in well-being all, on balance, make the union less necessary or less powerful or both. The conclusion seems inevitable. The union belongs to a particular stage in the development of the industrial system. When that stage passes so does the union in anything like its original position of power. And, as an added touch of paradox, things for which the unions fought vigorously—the regulation of aggregate demand to insure full employment and higher real income for members— have contributed to their decline.[14]

Adapting to the demands of the new industrial system and representing the knowledge worker rather than the laborer, whose group will probably continue to decrease both in numbers and as a percentage of the total workforce (technical and professional workers increased to 44.5 percent of the labor force by 1965 whereas they accounted for only 17.6 percent in 1900) could mean survival and growth for the unions. However, this would require that they become more like professional associations, performing the functions and offering the services of this type of organization. One of their principal objectives should be to help provide on their own and through collective bargaining the means by which their membership can keep up with changes in their work.

The increased training requirements of continuing high employment may be expected to become more of a preoccupation of collective bargaining. It is possible to envisage a day when supplemental agreements on training will be common to individual large-scale work places, or they will be developed on an industry or locality basis for smaller scale plants.[15]

If it had been the policy of the unions in the past to apply collective bargaining in this way, many independent associations—such as those whose membership comes from the relatively new medical

[14] John K. Galbraith, *The New Industrial State* (Boston, Houghton Mifflin Company, 1967), p. 274. Chapters 23 and 24 provide a concise but very effective analysis of the current and prospective state of unions in the American economy.
[15] Dunlop, *op. cit.*, p. 124.

knowledge worker (for example, the X-ray or laboratory technician)—might have found union membership more attractive and convenient than forming their own organizations.

The paradox is that the achievement of the long-term union objective of freeing the employee of the burden of labor has made union membership less appealing to the modern-day worker, for it has very little to offer this new breed. The words of Ralph Helstein, president of the United Packinghouse Workers, as quoted in the Chicago *Sun Times* of December 18, 1965, are very revealing:

> I tell my people they should not have to do the work they are doing; it is inhuman. And they agree with me. No man should have to stick pigs at the rate of one every 12 seconds, for instance, and the same can be said for the work of steelworkers, auto workers, and many others. Work as we know it is destroying man's best purpose.... I would teach everyone Shakespeare. I would teach them everything that perfects them as human beings. Basically I want a society to which every man's most important work will be understanding his life.... I am not interested in the concept of redistributing the wealth; that is academic and not very meaningful. But I am interested in making the economy truly full and truly competitive.[16]

In essence, the unions have worked themselves out of a job, aided by the rapid advance in technology. It will be well for them to change their objectives now to conform with the change in the concept of work—and to provide avenues for meeting the wants and needs of the knowledge worker. If they do not, employees will turn to other types of organizations to fill the vacuum brought about by their new status and new requirements for proficiency and employability.

Neil W. Chamberlain, in his very pertinent essay "What's Ahead for Labor?" states: "... Until genuine career planning for the future substitutes for makeshift efforts to hang onto present job opportunities, the unions will continue resolutely to face the past."[17] He goes on to state:

16 As quoted in *Education and Training for Full Employment*, by Seymour L. Wolfbein (New York, Columbia University Press, 1967), p. 22.

17 Neil W. Chamberlain, "What's Ahead for Labor?" *The Atlantic*, July 1964, p. 35. Copyright © 1965, by The Atlantic Monthly Company, Boston, Mass. 02116. Reprinted with permission.

The asset revolution has not yet touched the unions. When it does, as it must in time if they are to survive, they will be driven to adopt the same asset orientation that management has learned to live with and profit from. The lifetime careers of their members will be recognized as something for which short-run and long-run plans must be made. They will anticipate the obsolescence of skills—before obsolescence has destroyed the value of existing assets—by planning for a continuing metamorphosis of old skills into new. This can be done only by explicit attention to career development through programs designed to upgrade the general abilities and specific qualifications of their members. They will recognize that their members' welfare is not secured by attempting to hold on to present rights, growing out of past service, but by projecting a present position into some competence to be realized in the future. . . . The desperate search for ways of retaining market outlets for job abilities which are less and less wanted and needed will give way to a more rewarding examination of ways in which on-the-job training coupled with off-the-job educational opportunities can give their members qualifications which are continuously in demand.[18]

Consulting Services

The difficulty of maintaining a competent workforce has brought about increased interest in training programs developed by companies and associations organized for such purposes. There is no doubt that this interest will grow as the problems of providing for continuing employee effectiveness become more complex.

These firms and their programs have much to offer. They profit from experience and specialization, which most companies do not have or cannot afford to develop. They certainly should be consulted, particularly by those organizations that do not have personnel able to shape and implement new training concepts or whose closeness to problems obscures the issues involved and handicaps thoughtful analysis and the application of effective remedial action by personnel within the organization. Since training and other aspects of worker proficiency are the principal raison d'etre of these firms, their services can often be less expensive than company-

18 *Ibid.,* pp. 35–36.

organized projects and programs, especially when the specific need to be filled is of an infrequent or nonrecurring nature.

Success in using outside consulting services or "canned" training programs depends in large part on the approach to their use. There is always the temptation to press the panic button and call in outside help to handle a problem situation that can be solved only by the company itself. The training staff can then attempt to bolster its security by placing the blame for failure on the outsiders. Management must of course ascertain that the service or program being considered, particularly if it is of a specialized nature, is applicable to the situation faced by the company. In other words, the problem must first be defined; and, if the company feels that outside assistance will be of benefit, a firm with experience in that trouble area can be retained. In those situations where the problem is obscure and its nature difficult to ascertain, a consultant with a reputation for a basic, general approach should be called in.

Too often it has happened that, in desperation, company personnel—not knowing what else to do—have jumped to unwarranted conclusions and hired a consulting service or made use of programs that were not applicable to the situation they faced. The result has naturally been confusion and disappointment—and an aggravated training problem. A satisfactory solution will be even more remote if blame is cast on consulting in general and management reverts to the use of internal resources which are not adequate to the situation. The more logical approach is to recognize the original errors, attack the problem again from a new point of view, and employ assistance better fitted to the company needs and circumstances.

7

Responsibility
for Company Retraining

THE DRAMATIC CHANGE IN THE NATURE OF WORK—VERY OFTEN necessitating the learning of one or more completely new skills in a lifetime—has brought about considerable interest in retraining. It is not only that change is having an effect on worker status and proficiency; of greater significance is the fact that change can be expected to be a continuing occurrence, increasing in momentum and impact. In this kind of job climate, it is no longer the case, as was the situation until relatively recent times, that the learning of a skill implies job security and continuing ability to cope with a job assignment.

> ... Technological and market changes have tended to kill the security in occupational identity. The worker can depend less and less on retaining his occupational identity throughout his working career. He has less and less to gain from thinking of him-

self as a "spinner," a "loom tender," or even a "textile man." The new occupational identities, based on functions which cut across traditional industry categories, have only begun to be invented.[1]

For the purposes of this book, retraining will be defined as training needed to handle effectively a new job or learn a new skill which is not related to the work formerly performed by the employee concerned. Upgrading will not be considered as retraining. Although the emphasis will be on *company* retraining, much of the subject matter should be applicable to retraining in general, regardless of the sponsor. Certainly, whether it is a question of business, government, or any other organization, indications are that retraining will be increasingly costly, time consuming, and burdensome unless training takes on a new look; that is, a different philosophy and direction. To state the problem in another way, the day is fast approaching in many organizations when it may well be necessary to give greater emphasis to retraining than to training.

What must be done to avoid this situation is to institute training concepts, like those discussed previously, part of whose objective it is to minimize the necessity for retraining by facilitating continuing worker adaptability to the jobs to be performed, whatever they may be. Retraining, as it is presently defined and viewed, is often no more than attacking a symptom; it fails to do very much about alleviating the worker status and problems which indicated the need for action in the first place. Chances are that this approach will demand continuous retraining efforts, which will never develop the kind of employee who has the ability to adapt quickly and economically to changing work situations and has been given incentives and aids to some degree of self-training.

This is not to imply that retraining is not advisable in some situations. But to depend on it as a principal avenue for achieving a capable, efficient workforce will neither be economical nor produce the best results. Moreover, it can seriously impede the progress of the enterprise. If an organization looks upon retraining as a major panacea for worker obsolescence, clearly it has not come to grips with the demands of its environment and has not developed a

1 Donald A. Schon, *Technology and Change* (New York, Delacorte Press, 1967), p. 195.

training attitude and philosophy which are compatible with the times. Eventually, a company's lack of need for a great number of formal retraining programs may be the chief yardstick in judging training effectiveness, for this will demonstrate that the organization is following a policy which enables its workers to maintain their proficiency regardless of any change in the makeup of their work.[2]

The Status of Retraining

There is always the tendency to be impatient with new concepts, to expect too much from them too soon, to give up too easily, and—finally—to throw up one's hands in despair because no easy way out is apparent. This is often the case in retraining. Those who look at it in this way fail to recognize that it is a relatively new kind of undertaking and, like all pursuits that are being given emphasis for the first time, it requires the willingness to experiment, the recognition that useless effort will often result before a body of knowledge is built up, the fortitude to stay with the task without giving up, and the persistence required to explore new ideas and new avenues of possible accomplishment continually.

What should be kept in mind is that retraining was almost unheard of, never even thought to be worthy of consideration, until the late 1950's and early 1960's. Very little was published on the subject before this time, and its short history has been plagued with faulty assumptions, skepticism, and an unfortunate absence of positive determination backed with sufficient resources. Time, experience, money, and well-thought-out effort are required to obtain fruitful results in any new venture—and not enough of these requisites for accomplishment have been applied to retraining to justify the negative attitude that it is of no use. Admittedly, it entails difficult problems, it can be a source of bitter disappointment, and it

---

[2] One of the recommendations resulting from the Armour Fund retraining experience is that "a carefully planned continuous education program, promoted and supported by both the company and the union, would help employees develop abilities and skills which would improve their positions in the labor market in a time of crisis." See "Progress Report of Armour's Tripartite Automation Committee," *Monthly Labor Review*, August 1961, p. 852.

is no substitute for continuous training. But the need today is obvious. In many organizations retraining is essential because of the unavailability of basic skills in the labor market and the organization's previous failure to keep employees abreast of change so that they can adapt readily to new work requirements. For example, although long-range planning and goal setting are common practice in most organizations, it is the exceptional firm that uses these tools to determine worker requirements in advance and make suitable preparations for meeting them.

In other words, until the concept of continuous training is operating effectively, there will probably be no alternative, in many cases, to a considerable retraining effort. Even where a policy of continuous training has been effectively implemented, there will be some need for retraining programs owing to the difficulty of predicting occupational needs exactly and the unlikelihood of being able to structure a continuous-type program that will meet all possible contingencies.

Advantages Too Often Overlooked

The gloom which very often surrounds retraining has acted as a barrier to sound thinking about its very real benefits. There are many. In addition to being, at times, the only means of securing qualified workers, retraining company employees who have been displaced by changes in technology and company operations also gives the workforce a greater sense of loyalty and security. Knowing that their employer is sufficiently concerned about their welfare to provide a means of insuring their continuing employability is bound to instill in employees a new feeling toward the organization and result in the peace of mind that is conducive to increased productivity. And the fact that word of the company's concern is bound to spread throughout the community should help to attract the best-qualified job applicants.

Another advantage is that existing employees usually have proved their reliability. Their work habits and attitudes about the job and the company are known; and, if they have worked effectively at one task, they have indicated that they possess all the traits—except technical proficiency—to be competent in another.

In addition, their capabilities, aptitudes, character traits, and potential for development—all the factors, in short, which determine proficiency—are more of a certainty than is the case with prospective new employees. Taking the total view of the displaced employee, judging him on the basis of these many attributes which affect productivity—rather than simply looking at the cost and effort of retraining—should weigh heavily in his favor when attempting to choose between retraining or hiring qualified outsiders.

Nor should it be overlooked that existing employees are already familiar with the company's products, traditions, policies, and ways of doing things. The knowledge they have gained of the personality of the organization and its members aids in understanding company behavior and in developing productive relationships with other employees and with management. This accumulated store of knowledge is an asset that only time and experience can provide.

Yet the positive qualifications of the displaced employee are not usually given full consideration in reaching a decision on retraining. Management forgets that outsiders who are brought in to take new jobs, although they may be technically qualified, will still require considerable training in company policies, philosophy, and methodology. Actually, they are in the same position as is the displaced worker: they are only partly qualified from the standpoint of the full range of attributes demanded for satisfactory job performance.

There is also the question of moral obligation to long-service employees, particularly if they have been faithful to their work and their inability to adjust to change is due to no fault of their own. If any blame is to be cast, perhaps the employer should bear much of it for failing to foresee developments affecting worker proficiency, and for not providing the assistance necessary to permit employees to adapt to changing work requirements. To dismiss these men and women simply because their jobs are being eliminated by new processes requiring different qualifications is bound to have a negative effect on the outlook of all company personnel toward the organization. If this becomes accepted policy, the image developed can be one of a company that is "not a good place to work." Recruiting efforts will be jeopardized, and it will be difficult to retain the above-average worker. And adverse opinion on the part of both the public and the private sectors of the community can have an undesirable effect on company sales and profits.

All these arguments in favor of retraining are usually minimized because they are not easily turned into dollars-and-cents cost figures. It very often appears to be simpler and more economical to hire workers who are already trained or, it is thought, will be more readily trainable. But this can be an elusively false notion based on a one-sided view of the situation which is frequently colored by assumptions and hearsay, and any policy based on it can actually result in greater long-term costs to the organization than the costs of retraining. Difficult though it is to place a value on the advantages of retraining displaced workers, this must be done if a well-grounded and valid decision is to be reached.

Company Retraining Efforts Meager

Although there has been a great deal of talk on the subject, all the evidence indicates that well-planned action is the exception. Ida R. Hoos concludes:

> A survey of industry has uncovered the fact that retraining on a large scale for workers threatened with skill obsolescence is rarely undertaken. Courses in safety practices, salesmanship, and management development prevail among industry-sponsored endeavours. Indoctrination and orientation are commonplace; specialized instructions given by the equipment vendors is a favoured practice. But programmes specifically designed to provide employees with new skills for job security in anticipation of technological change are exceedingly infrequent.[3]

When retraining programs are undertaken, they are not usually accepted as a significant affirmation of company policy and, consequently, do not rank very high in the hierarchy of things to be accomplished. They are given attention after everything else is taken care of, and the result is often a hodgepodge of methodology without scientific planning and research into the peculiarities of the problems involved. Delay and procrastination may reach the

---

3 Ida R. Hoos, "Retraining in the United States: Problems and Progress," *The International Labor Review*, November 1965, p. 414. The author refers to the U.S. Department of Labor's *Training Workers in American Industry* (Washington, Government Printing Office, 1964) as the source of her conclusion.

point where a crash program must be undertaken, with all the weaknesses the term implies.

It follows that when retraining is handled in this way, the resources allocated for its implementation are often insufficient to support an effective program. Even when it is approached with dedication and seriousness of purpose, there exists the tendency to underestimate the magnitude and complexity of the undertaking and, therefore, fail to devote adequate funds, facilities, and personnel to the project. It is reported that the U.S. Office of Vocational Rehabilitation was not in the least surprised with the disappointment resulting from the original Armour Fund experience. The Fund had allocated no more than $150 per retrainee to the project, whereas the Office was spending, at the time, an average of $2,000 to counsel, train, and place each individual in its program.

It is only natural that when retraining is not given real status in the organization, supervisory forces will tend to direct their attention and efforts to what they believe to be more pressing matters. This will make it very difficult for retraining to succeed, since the willing cooperation of the supervisory level is needed to adjust production plans and goals to allow for retraining and to help encourage and motivate the employees concerned. If retraining is not given the needed emphasis, it can even happen that when a production process or type of work is being phased out, those employees who have been the least cooperative and proficient will be the first released by the supervisor for retraining—in the interests of keeping the better workers so as to establish as good a productivity record as possible. Where this is common practice, the effectiveness of the program is judged on the basis of those who were least qualified to benefit from it. Consequently, the desire of the organization to continue retraining is impaired, and retraining opportunities for those who are most likely to benefit are delayed or denied.

Approach Lacks Originality

Although retraining is different from training, it is very often conducted in accordance with the staid principles and practices which the training department has found to be applicable in its regular training activities. The special problems which retraining presents, and the need for special methodology, have seldom been given the consideration necessary to develop a realistic program. Efforts have also been thwarted by assumptions which are not invariably based on fact. "You can't teach an old dog new tricks," "They really don't want to learn anything new," "They're satisfied as they are and don't care to make any progress" are remarks which we hear over and over when the subject of retraining comes up for discussion. Moreover, such statements frequently become accepted conclusions without any real effort to determine their validity or their wholesale applicability. They are simply excuses to justify a negative attitude on the part of management and training department personnel.

There is evidence to indicate that some of the assumptions and thoughts about retraining are far from universally valid. For example, the data gathered by R. M. Belbin on retraining the older worker (this is the age grouping in which most prospective retrainees fall) tend to throw a different light on the oftentimes accepted premise that there is a decline in learning performance, due to age, which begins around 40. Belbin concludes that experimental studies leading to this hypothesis should be looked at with considerable caution for the following reasons:

1. Experimental studies of learning have often been based on highly artificial tasks, chosen to minimize the effect of prior knowledge in the learning situation. It has been established, however, that older adults react unfavorably to being presented with tasks that appear to them strange and meaningless. Thus some of the apparent decline in performance is known to be a function of reaction to the nature of the material.

2. Older persons are usually out of practice in learning. Measurements, therefore, refer largely to initial or immediate ability rather than to potential learning ability.

3. The majority of studies on human learning ability have been carried out without any attempt being made to

adapt the method of training and instruction to the needs of the older subject.[4]

Belbin goes on to say that the evidence he has examined supports the generalization:

In cases where no special consideration is given to the problems of the middle-aged adult, there is a tendency for performance and ultimate attainment to decline sharply from various ages ranging from the late twenties to the fifties. But where training methods are adapted to the needs of adults in the middle age range, the relationship between age and performance is seldom marked: differences in ultimate attainment may usually be offset by an extension in training time.[5]

Among the cases cited by Belbin are the following:

RETRAINING OF OIL REFINERY PRODUCTION WORKERS

Eighty-two production workers were given retraining to prepare them for work in a modernized and highly automated oil refinery. Retraining was carried out in full-time courses lasting several weeks. Information on the performance of trainees was obtained from grades received in written examinations. This information showed that a high proportion of trainees over the age of forty received below average grades. But the differences in attainment between age groups were very nearly eliminated when comparison was confined to trainees having the same number of years of formal schooling.

In the same company, retraining was also provided for 18 instrument mechanics in courses involving theoretical and practical training over a period of nine months. The differences between younger and older trainees in examination accomplishment at the

---

[4] R. M. Belbin, *Training Methods for Older Workers* (Paris, Organization for Economic Co-operation and Development, 1965), p. 65. Together with *Accelerated Vocational Training for Adults*, by Victor Martin, also published by OECD, this publication contains useful information and suggests effective methods for training the older worker.

[5] *Ibid.*, p. 66.

end of the course were small, with a slight tendency for trainees over forty to obtain higher performances on certain divisions of the examination material.

RETRAINING OF AIRCRAFT PRODUCTION WORKERS,
TECHNICIANS, AND ENGINEERS

A large aircraft manufacturing company, having experienced difficulty in recruiting persons with requisite skills, established a large training department with over 100 employees and succeeded in obtaining 90 per cent of their skilled personnel by taking inexperienced employees and training them upwards through a succession of skills. Courses included optical tooling for assemblers, electronics for engineers and technical writers, blueprint reading for machinists, and advanced welding for those with previous welding experience.

The results obtained were broadly similar to those found in the oil refinery. There was a slight tendency for those over forty to pass with a lower than average grade, but this tendency virtually disappeared when differences in the educational level of trainees were taken into account. In welding, the average time taken to qualify was slightly longer than for younger trainees.

RETRAINING OF AIRLINE MAINTENANCE MECHANICS

The replacement of piston-engined aircraft by those powered by turbine engines and jets has entailed extensive retraining of maintenance personnel. A study was carried out in one company in which 1,200 workers were retrained. These courses were divided into six levels according to their technical complexity. The first level entailed only 8 hours training while the sixth entailed 240 hours. Analysis of the performance of trainees showed that of those taking the first level only, older trainees did better than young trainees. However, on the remaining course levels the average performance of older trainees proved somewhat inferior to the average performance of younger trainees.[6]

6 Ibid., pp. 36-37.

Very much the same kind of conclusions resulted from retraining conducted by the International Business Machines Corporation for the job of computer system technician.

An exploratory study designed to determine the feasibility of retraining employees made surplus or technologically obsolete indicated that, if necessary, many of the employees previously not considered eligible could be retrained for a relatively high-level technician's job. It was found that learning ability did not present a major obstacle but that the educational background of the employees (and particularly their knowledge of mathematics and technical subjects) was a definite limiting factor. Employee acceptance of the opportunity to enroll in the retraining program seemed to be influenced by their interest in the work, confidence in their ability to succeed, and the climate created by management. Finally, the number of employees in this situation considered not suitable for any type of retraining was estimated to be very small provided that the training time, when necessary, was increased with a resulting increase in cost per trained employee.[7]

All evidence indicates that retraining can be feasible and that it can be successful if we recognize that it is a special type of problem requiring understanding of its nature and peculiarities and of the necessity for using applicable training methodology. As the IBM experience reveals, its acceptance by employees is "influenced by their interest in their work, confidence in their ability to succeed, and the climate created by management." In essence, its success or failure is determined primarily by the ability of management, particularly first-line supervisors and training department, to create the necessary interest, build the needed confidence, and provide a positive framework for carrying out the program. Prospective re-

[7] Walter J. McNamara, "Retraining of Industrial Personnel," *Personnel Psychology*, Autumn 1963, p. 247. The description for the job of computer system technician reads: "Tests and analyzes highly complex electronic computer systems to determine acceptability from standpoint of performance and physical qualities. Follows established test procedure to check out all possible operations on the system. When an error, failure, or malfunction is encountered, uses knowledge of theory and design of system to diagnose cause of malfunction. Takes or describes proper corrective action. Completely responsible for functional quality of the computer system. Instructs and guides less qualified technicians in test procedures and analysis of system malfunctions." *Ibid.*, p. 234.

trainees are too often expected to supply these elements of success on their own; but it should be apparent that this is not very likely to happen, nor is it practical to expect good results if retrainees are treated as if they were new trainees.

Developing a Retraining Policy

To repeat: There will probably always be situations in organizations which demand that consideration be given to the feasibility of retraining, even where an effective continuous training concept is in force and tends to keep special requirements at a minimum. How should an organization go about determining the policy which it should follow on retraining? The first step is to look at the problem of job displacement and the need for new skills from an overall point of view. It may not be the best solution to conclude immediately that displaced workers should be retrained, for it may be possible to assign them to jobs which do not call for retraining and obtain required skills from outside the organization. Alternately, other employees in the company may have better qualifications for retraining in the needed skills, and the displaced workers may adapt more easily to the jobs of those so qualified. What should be avoided is the tendency to look at worker displacement as automatically calling for intensive retraining. Other solutions may be available which would be more acceptable and beneficial to both the employees concerned and the organization.

The qualifications of training department personnel in the area of retraining and the availability of facilities are other matters to be considered in the formulation of retraining policy. Since retraining is a unique kind of undertaking, it should not be assumed without investigation that existing training personnel and facilities will be adequate. Retraining personnel should have a deep understanding of its nature and special problems. They should be particularly cognizant of the social-psychological attitudes of retrainees, their fears and aspirations, and their sensitivity about their status. These characteristics of retrainees, along with the methods they call for, make retraining somewhat different from regular training and the usual development of workers; therefore, retraining may be a difficult task for the average training department to cope with successfully. If any doubt exists as to its ability to handle the situation, the best approach may be to bring in consultants to set up the initial programs, conduct the sessions, and train personnel to meet future needs. Vendors who have had experience in this field may also be called upon for advice in getting a program under way.

Qualified personnel may very well be found among workers who have been successfully retrained. Having lived through the experience of their prospective students, they should be especially sensitive to their particular problems and status and hence more sympathetic and understanding—two traits which are most desirable for the retraining staff to possess. Not all retrainees will be acceptable, of course, but there are bound to be some who are exceptionally intelligent, articulate, adaptable, and suited in other basic respects to participation in retraining programs. The possibility of using them as administrators, advisers, and instructors should not be overlooked.

Proposed action in the area of retraining must naturally consider the cost factor.[8] This requires an evaluation of the job for which the workers are to be retrained and the degree to which they may be considered susceptible to retraining. It is only after this determination has been made that the program needed and the effort required can be estimated, translated into terms of costs, and related to the anticipated monetary return of the expected results.

The inclination is to consider the cost factor without attention to the development of worker traits which will permit continuous training so that the retrained employees will not be so subject in the future to obsolescence. Also, there is the tendency to place little emphasis on the numerous subjective advantages of retraining pointed out earlier in this chapter. Yet no valid assessment of the situation should leave out the long-term benefits—including the

---

[8] For a study of the cost factor in retraining from the standpoint of the economy see Michael E. Borus, "The Economic Effectiveness of Retraining the Unemployed," *Research Report to the Federal Reserve Bank of Boston,* No. 35, July 1966. The purpose of this study was "to weigh the benefits and costs of the retraining programs to determine if retraining is a sound investment for the individual worker, the government, and the economy" (p. 3). On the basis of sample data, Mr. Borus concludes: "The benefits of retraining outweigh its cost to the individual, to the government, and to the economy. The high benefit-cost ratios enjoyed by each party suggest that retraining should be extended. Given the present costs of the program, as many workers as possible should be retrained for occupations with labor shortages because the net returns from retraining are so great" (p. 85).

minimization of future retraining costs—to be brought about by incorporating in retraining programs subject matter and methodology which will prepare employees for continuous training. Nor should cost analysis fail to take into consideration the asset value to the organization of long-service employees as well as the positive impact on morale which can result from employer concern for the worker demonstrated through the medium of retraining.

Even if costs appear to be excessive in relation to the benefits to be derived, retraining (or at least finding some place in the company for the displaced worker) can still be a desirable practice. It is the general belief that the Maximum Employment Act makes labor a cost to be borne by the business organization whether people are working or idle. John Bunting alludes to this when he says, "Now there is every good economic reason for business to assume everyone in the labor force as a fixed cost. After all, what this Act means is that each person in the labor force is to be employed or to receive income while temporarily unemployed. One way or another, business is going to pay labor whether working or not."[9] It follows that even though retraining displaced employees may be costly and they may not produce as much as they are being paid, it may still be less expensive to retrain than to release them and have to bear the burden of their unemployment through higher taxes.

Another major factor to consider in determining retraining policy is the organization's sense of its responsibility to the worker and to society. It would be difficult to pose as a responsible employer, in the modern sense of the word, without providing for the continuing employability of the workforce—particularly of those workers with some seniority. For society is concluding nowadays that, in an increasing number of situations, employers have some obligation to rehabilitate workers when the need arises. Failure to recognize this obligation will adversely affect the way the organization is viewed by prospective employees, public bodies, and the general public.

There is no doubt that as time goes by, and business organizations become more and more social in nature, they will be penalized or rewarded by the workforce and by public pressure reflected through government attitude on the basis of their being adept at handling problems—such as retraining—which reflect on the health

9 John R. Bunting, "What's Ahead for Business?" *The Atlantic*, June 1964, p. 72.

of the economy and the dignity of the citizenry. In other words, a positive attitude toward retraining may be the only real choice open to the astute and wise employer who is conscious of the demanding environment in which business establishments operate and which transforms them into socially responsible as well as business-oriented organizations. At the same time, caution should be exercised in looking at retraining solely from the standpoint of responsibility. For, when emotional impact, rather than sound reasoning, is the principal determinant in developing retraining plans, the result may be impractical and costly programs which do not produce the desired effects.

Retraining can become somewhat of a fad, in which case it may be carried out without much thought or planning. It can also be put into practice simply on the basis that it is the acceptable procedure to follow and the expected thing to do. But, just as when a sense of responsibility toward one's employees provides the main reason for retraining, the instinct to be in fashion and adhere to what is thought to be expected practice often leads management to minimize the need to scrutinize the practical aspects of retraining and its feasibility. What must be kept in mind is that retraining is not easy to handle successfully and efficiently; it requires careful study and planning. To allow emotional, sentimental, or follow-the-leader principles to be the major guidelines in formulating retraining policy will, in most cases, mean an ineffective and costly policy.

The Retraining Program in Practice

There are so many variables to consider in putting retraining into practice that it is impractical to establish a set pattern to follow. Each situation will demand individual attention and require a particular approach. It is highly probable that many retraining projects have not achieved the planned-for success simply because those in charge failed to recognize the peculiarities of the situation and tailor their program accordingly. Instead, they put into effect, in toto and without study, concepts which had worked for other organizations or had been effective in prior company retraining situations.

The workers to be retrained, the job for which they are to be prepared, and the method and approach to be used are the three major areas to be studied in developing a retraining program.

The worker and the work. The first question to be answered is whether or not those being considered for retraining have basic qualifications which will permit them to be retrained and, if not, whether they can be provided with the essential requisites. (The literature on the subject is in general agreement that lack of a basic education is more of a deterrent to retraining than age.) For example, some skills may require an understanding of mathematics and physics; so, if such knowledge is lacking, the first steps in the direction of retraining should be directed at insuring comprehension in these areas. However, it may be that the workers concerned are not capable of assimilating this necessary background knowledge in an acceptable manner. If this is the case, it is futile to retrain them in these skills. The more sensible approach is to try to find other jobs for which these prospective retrainees have the basic qualifications or for which they can be taught the essential background information.

Experience indicates that related skills are nowhere near as important as the possession of some previous skill. Workers who have such a skill are much more likely to be successfully retrained for another, regardless of its relation to their previous occupation. The Air Force Logistics Command has found that "skilled and semi-skilled workers frequently cross the line between blue and white collar, or make switches as sweeping as that from propeller repairman to electronics specialist. . . ."[10] It is generally agreed, also, that it is impractical to attempt to retrain unskilled workers for skill-type jobs, particularly if the workers concerned have been employed in an unskilled capacity for some time. Employment in the unskilled category of the workforce may be a strong indication that a worker does not have the educational background required to grasp the basic knowledge necessary for effective performance in a new skill, or that he lacks the ambition and determination needed to improve his status.

Another factor, very often overlooked, is the desire of the worker to be retrained. It has happened that retraining programs

10 "Where Job Retraining Works," *Business Week,* June 23, 1962, pp. 49–52.

organized after determining that workers met the necessary mental and physical requirements have not been successful simply because the workers did not want to be retrained or would not contribute the effort necessary. It therefore follows that prospective retrainees, in addition to being examined for mental and physical qualifications, must also be scrutinized to determine their interest and willingness to cooperate. Only if all of these requisites are present can it be expected that a well-thought-out and sensibly administered program will bear fruit. Many companies have found that a counseling program can aid in matching qualifications with the retraining program and help allay the psychological fears of the retrainee.

> ... The performance of those few workers provided counseling suggests that such procedures might lead to better matching of the candidates' aptitudes with the retraining to be given and modification of programs to meet the needs of the trainees. Counseling also helps allay apprehensions about training, especially for older workers who may resist training because of its novelty or unfamiliarity.[11]

The selection process also presents unique problems. In a report on the experience of 20 companies that introduced large-scale computers requiring the retraining of personnel for their operation, it was found that

> ... The administration of suitable aptitude tests in selecting a staff was a critical problem. Many of the workers in the affected units were unwilling to expose their knowledge, or lack thereof, in the visible context of a test that would be known to their supervisors. This was particularly true for the older, long-term workers.[12]

Retraining methodology. Since workers to be retrained are usually older employees, or younger employees who must be retrained because of gaps in their educational background, retraining pre-

11 "Older Workers' Performance in Industrial Retraining Programs," *Monthly Labor Review,* August 1963, p. 936.
12 Edward B. Jakubauskas, "Retraining Problems Created Through Equipment Replacement," *Personnel Journal,* November 1963, p. 516.

sents some special problems which demand that considerable attention be given to the approaches to be used to facilitate the learning
process and get the cooperation of the retrainees. This is not to say
that those selected for retraining do not have to learn as much as
any other workers in a specific skill in order to be proficient; however, they have to be taught and directed through the learning
experience in a somewhat different way. What must be borne in
mind is that they have undergone a rather traumatic experience in
discovering that their ability to be productive in their occupation
has come to an end.

Younger workers, who have not achieved the educational norm
expected by society for their group, may tend to be very insecure
and, as a result, appear unenthusiastic and noncooperative. They
hesitate to expose themselves to what they believe could be an
embarrassing situation for them. In all probability, they have
experienced educational situations which resulted in failure and
unhappiness; thus they may actually resent the prospect of undertaking yet another effort which they may feel can only result in a
repetition of past humiliations.

Older workers may have reached a degree of satisfaction with
their skill and status and may also be concerned about their ability
to grasp new concepts. The process of retraining can be particularly
distressing to this group if they feel that they may be placed in a
situation (for example, with younger, better-educated workers)
where they will find it difficult to keep up with the rest and where
the little confidence which they have in themselves may be destroyed. The seniority system may be so structured that older
workers do not have to worry about technological change to enjoy
job security and so find little reason to be cooperative. Probably
they have endured numerous setbacks and still survived; in any
case they have become conditioned to accepting their position and
are disinclined to seek a change.[13]

The training methods used should avoid placing these workers
in situations which could be embarrassing to them or under conditions with which they feel they cannot cope. They must first be
assured of their ability to grasp the new skill and be firmly con-

[13] Ned A. Rosen, Lawrence K. Williams, and F. F. Foltman, "Motivational Con-
straints in an Industrial Retraining Program," *Personnel Psychology*, Spring 1965,
pp. 65-79.

vinced that they will not encounter emotional and social-psychological difficulties. What are some guidelines to follow?

▪ Avoid training different age, social, and educational levels together in the same group. Retraining is much more likely to be successful if the group is homogeneous, if the members feel that all are of the same status with the same fears, problems, and anxieties. This will also facilitate the organization of the training program, since it can be aimed at a group with similar background, experience, and problems. Professor Otis Lipstreu states:

> Present evidence suggest that older workers often perform as well or better than younger workers when proper attention is given to age groupings and length of training time. If upgrading training is organized according to age groupings, several other facets of the adjustment of older, more experienced workers can be dealt with more effectively. For example, it is difficult for this group to accept new concepts of how to run machines. For them to learn to keep their hands off and to leave adjustments to skilled maintenance technicians is exceedingly painful. Furthermore, the art of instructing experienced, older employees so as to minimize their tendencies to override automatic controls manually requires careful, sympathetic attention from the trainer, since again lack of understanding of the basic problem can blunt learning speed.[14]

▪ Unless the circumstances are very unusual, it would appear inadvisable to group trainees and retrainees together in the same training program. These are two entirely different groups, demanding different approaches to achieve the desired results.
▪ Instruction should be conducted with more in mind than just the objective of getting the material over to the retrainees. It should also have as its purpose the building of confidence, the avoidance of embarrassment, and the

[14] Otis Lipstreu, "Problem Areas in Training for Automated Work." Reprinted by special permission from the November 1964 issue of the *Training Directors Journal* (now *Training and Development Journal*). Copyright 1964 by the American Society for Training and Development.

assurance of accomplishment. For example, it may be best to start at a level of the subject matter that is already well known to the retrainees so that they will get the feeling that they are on safe ground and will be able to understand what is to follow. Another useful procedure, which could be instituted at the beginning of the training period, is to have a question box in which the retrainees can deposit inquiries that they may be reluctant to make outwardly during the sessions. These need not be answered directly; instead, the answers can be made part of the instruction (provided those being instructed are made to understand that this is the way in which their inquiries will be handled). Retraining is usually a delicate undertaking, and greater progress can be made if it is approached with a view to sparing the feelings of the participants as much as possible.

■ The material to be used, as well as its sequence, should be carefully thought out in terms of the group's learning level. This means that the same course content and structure may not be applicable to different groups of retrainees, even though they are being retrained for the same purposes. Each group has to be looked at from the standpoint of the people who make it up.

■ If there is any indication that comprehension is wanting, the instructor should go back over the last point of understanding before reemphasizing and further explaining the point of difficulty. This should be done without letting the group know of the reason for this procedure. In essence, everything possible should be done to avoid having the retrainees develop the feeling that they are not grasping the subject matter in accordance with the planned schedule. The material and method of instruction, rather than the worker, should be blamed if difficulties arise.

■ As often as possible and prudent, the group should be complimented on its achievement in order to build up its poise and confidence.

■ Some procedure should be devised for individual instruction without making its purpose apparent. Even with groups of like attributes, there will be problems of comprehension that can be handled only on an individual basis. Using teaching machines, with an instructor present for consultation, can both permit the trainee to progress at his own pace and provide a source of information to clear up possible areas and points of confusion.[15]

Retraining should be recognized for what it is: a very difficult, specialized, and expensive practice. Even the guidelines offered here will work only if the retrainees' mental and physical status and their emotional level are in accord with the objectives of the particular retraining program. It should also be recognized that a retraining project cannot really be termed successful unless it conditions the individuals being retrained to take advantage of the concepts of continuous and total training. If this is not the case, these same retrainees will have to be retrained again at least once, and perhaps more often. This is a very costly and time-consuming solution to the problem of worker obsolescence—one which few organizations have the resources to endure.

[15] "Older persons show a marked preference for exercising some control over the rate at which they receive information and the rate at which they respond." Belbin, *op. cit.* p. 31.

8

The New Opportunities
for Industry

W<small>E ARE WITNESSING A NEW ERA IN TRAINING—MORE DEMANDING</small>
and difficult yet ever more challenging—brought about by
the evolving technological environment and the resulting emergence
of the professional-type employee, who performs a kind of work
which requires new attributes for proficiency and a different concept of supervision. But this is not all. Industry is also being sum-
moned to develop ways and means of enabling some members of
our society, who have become victims of the changed industrial
and social environment, to achieve the status of fruitful contribution. Because of background and deprivation resulting from upbringing and surroundings, and because of loss of motivation due to
disappointment—all stemming in part from the rapid change in
the nature of the economy and the new talents needed for productivity—this group is not being permitted to share in the affluence
of this nation.

The members of this group are in this condition, not because
this is their wish, but because change has come about so quickly

that it has not permitted them time for the kind of education and adjustment demanded by the new work requirements. What has happened to many of them is that they have entered into the age of technology and the knowledge worker directly from the 19th-century agricultural stage of the economy, without first participating in or reaping the benefits of the intermediate industrial phase of development. They are therefore behind the times and must be brought up to present standards of employability if they are to lead productive lives. The lives which they have been forced to lead have also deprived them of the chance to develop the industriousness, discipline, and other character traits needed to qualify for rewarding work. Hence we call them "the disadvantaged," or "the hard-core unemployed."

At the same time there is another group of our citizens who, although having the basic mental requisites and a background which should contribute to effectiveness, are on the brink of becoming future economic and behavioral problems because they are failing to complete at least a high school education owing to economic, emotional, or other problems. Helping these potential dropouts continue with their education and develop the character traits and other qualifications needed to insure their continuing employability is a challenge requiring a special training approach.

Third, the emergence of the multinational corporation, giving emphasis to industrial expansion outside domestic boundaries, has stirred inquiry and interest in the training of foreign workers. This is another field which presents special kinds of training problems, generally quite different from those encountered at the home base of the organization. Much of the success of operations in other countries will depend on bringing foreign workers to the point where they will develop work habits and practices which are in accord with established requirements, standards, and ways of doing things in the parent organization.

The Disadvantaged

Willing or not, business and industry have been assigned the task of aiding the disadvantaged in becoming productive and developing a sense of dignity by government officials, spokesmen for the disadvantaged, and the public itself. The responsibility vested in the business community is more than a request for assistance; it is a dare and a demand and—to many—the last hope of a successful solution to the problem. President Johnson has appealed to business leaders in these words: ". . . Help me find jobs for these people or we are going to have to offer every one of them a job in government." A black militant leader, speaking to Detroit businessmen, has issued the same challenge to them in more colorful terms: "If you cats can't do it, it's never going to get done. . . . The government can't lick this problem. . . . So business has to."[1] The Negro psychologist Kenneth B. Clark states, "Business and industry are our last hope. They are the most realistic elements of our society."[2]

To judge by these and other recent statements on the subject, knowledgeable and prominent authorities—including many businessmen—have seemingly come to the conclusion that business must play an important role in enabling the disadvantaged to find means by which they can lead useful lives. Max Ways in *Fortune* attests to this when he concludes:

> Business is the one important segment of society Negroes today do not regard with bitter disillusionment, and thousands of businessmen across the nation, getting involved in the struggle to restore social cohesion, are beginning to lift their sights, to sense that indeed business has a great part to play.[3]

And Theodore Levitt, in his article "Why Business Always Loses," reports:

> After a large national company's Los Angeles plant was virtually destroyed during the Watts riots, the president told a small gathering of industry executives, "Suddenly I saw we could close our eyes to this issue no longer. I went out and saw the ghetto, not because I had never been there, but because circumstances forced me to really *look* at what before I had only seen. It was appalling. If we do not straighten this matter out, we will be in an awful mess. We are going to get on board the civil rights thing

[1] "Business and the Urban Crisis," *Business Week*, February 3, 1968, p. C3.
[2] "What Business Can Do for the Negro," *Nation's Business*, October 1967, p. 67.
[3] Max Ways, "The Deeper Shame of the Cities," *Fortune*, January 1968, p. 132.

—and seriously. I will be the first to admit that we have been blind to the Negro problem in our company. It is because *I* have been blind. Well, that is over. We are going to do our part. If we do not, we will all go under."[4]

Business and industry, therefore, should no longer be deliberating the question of whether or not they should get involved. Rather, they should be determining what can be done. And an indication that they are doing so is the publication by the Chase Manhattan Bank of *Action Report,* a newsletter on business participation in solving public problems. Its objective is described by the bank's chairman, George Champion, in the first issue: "*Action Report* will describe what private companies are doing to solve many of the nation's social and economic problems. We hope this digest of corporate approaches will encourage businessmen and civic leaders everywhere to think in terms of a broader, more vigorous role for private enterprise."

One solution, of course, is training to facilitate the employment of the disadvantaged. This should not be looked upon solely as an obligation or responsibility. On the contrary, it can be an opportunity to get in on the ground floor of what, in the future, could be a major aspect of business activity and concern. There is increasing belief that in order to continue to prosper and in some instances survive, business is going to have to give as much attention to environmental and social research as it has given to research in science and technology. The ability to launch successful new products, respond to consumer desires, introduce better ways of doing things, redesign production processes, grasp worker values, and the like will be increasingly determined by an understanding of the changing environment and its effect on the individual, his outlook, and his habits. Advances and discoveries resulting from science and technology will no longer suffice to keep the company ahead or even abreast of the pack. Technological research will very shortly have to be matched with its environmental, social, and psychological equivalent if business is going to develop the knowledge needed to plan profitable courses of action and meaningful methods of operation and administration.

[4] Theodore Levitt, "Why Business Always Loses," *Harvard Business Review,* March-April 1968, p. 88.

The president of AT&T, Ben S. Gilmer, stated in a recent address:

> There are those in our business who see the need for nothing less than carefully organized, definitely expert, social research that will keep us fit to anticipate, or at the very least, keep up with, rapid changes in the environment that could otherwise leave a business wondering what in the world hit it. Fifty or more years ago, industry started moving in a substantial way toward research in the natural sciences. Out of this move, and the union of science and technology, came the advances that have produced both the benefits and also some of the problems we have today. Today, half a century later, the time may well be at hand when a business that hopes to survive and prosper will have no less a need for social and environmental research and planning than it had in the past for technical insights and expanding technical proficiency.[5]

A study of the disadvantaged and the environmental aspects of their situation, as well as their socio-psychological state, is necessary to the development of training methodology. It would also appear to be, for a number of organizations, the ideal area in which to begin the type of research which many businessmen feel is advisable for future corporate growth. Research in the area of training the disadvantaged to permit them to lead productive lives should not only yield a greater understanding of their plight and applicable methods of training; it should also produce new knowledge which could benefit training in general and environmental discoveries which would assist management in developing sound and timely direction for the business organization.

Not to be overlooked are the possibilities of needed breakthroughs in many unresolved areas of education, particularly the way in which people learn. These new discoveries not only would contribute to the education process, and thus help both the organization and society, but could very well result in salable ideas and profitable educational-type products. That this could be a significant opportunity is readily recognized when we remember that education is one of the largest and best-growing markets—one which has

[5] Ben S. Gilmer, "A Time for Action," address before the National Conference of Christians and Jews, December 1967, Denver, Colo.

been neglected from the standpoint of research and innovation and is in particular need of new ideas and products.

Also to be considered is the general expectation that government will as soon as feasible earmark substantially increased funds for dealing with the problems of the disadvantaged. From all indications, such expenditures will comprise one of the largest, if not the largest, segment of the federal budget, making it possible that the business of the disadvantaged will be the fastest-growing aspect of the economy. Organizations which have been early to develop interest and programs in training the disadvantaged stand most to profit from this inevitable outlay of funds. All of which serves to underscore the contention that getting involved in training the disadvantaged can best be defined as an *opportunity* rather than a *responsibility*.

There is mounting belief, too, that the potential growth of business cannot be achieved unless some solution is found to the urban crisis, and that a significant part of the answer lies in training members of the hard-core unemployed to become employable so that they can lead productive lives. This will not only add to the number of real consumers and taxpayers but will help in achieving that internal peace in the country which, obviously, is essential to profitable business activity. When people are able to lead productive lives, they are much less prone to become part of disturbing movements which can create problems for business and even disrupt the economy of an entire area or industry.

A leading business executive describes the challenge in these words:

> As must all other segments of society, business must realize that long-standing social wrongs have to be righted; we cannot hold ourselves aloof from the considerations of humanity and justice that rise from the urban problem. But we have added incentives for action, perhaps even more broadly beneficial in the long run because they rise from the basic nature of our national economy. There is no question that the good health, growth, and creative vitality of our private enterprise system depend on the soundness of our developing urban life. Business has an enormous stake in the city. A tremendous investment in plant, people, and market right now stands imperiled by the uncertainties of the urban future.

... Business also has the economic leverage to effect a basic change that must be effected in the quality of the urban ghetto life—it has jobs. And only when the ghetto resident gains the self-esteem that comes from a good and steady job—a job he knows he is filling satisfactorily—can we expect to see an end to his frustrations and the destructive negativism it has bred in our cities.[6]

The economics of the problem is more striking when it is recognized that there are a million jobless youngsters—most of them in urban centers—between the ages of 16 and 21. Each of these unemployed who remains in this status will end up costing the taxpayers —mainly business organizations and businessmen—$100,000, not including the loss to the economy of his potential productivity. Even if it costs $5,000 to $10,000 apiece to train members of this group effectively, the cost is small in relation to the price that will have to be paid for each of the hard-core unemployed who is not given the help he needs to find a way out of his situation.

If he is properly trained, the disadvantaged can then help to alleviate the shortages which now exist in many types of skills. Or if he is not suited to skilled or semiskilled work, he can perform the job of some other employee who is capable of being trained for a more demanding occupation.

The Nature of the Problem

Any person who requires a special kind of consideration, attention, and training in order to lead a productive life belongs to the classification of the disadvantaged. Although, because of poor environment and background, many in this group are Negroes, the inability to find gainful employment owing to inadequate qualifications or to personality, background, and character problems does not restrict itself solely to a particular race, creed, or geographical area. Inability to achieve an acceptable economic status results from one or, more likely, a combination of the following factors:

- Poor educational background.
- No concept of work or training.

[6] Ben S. Gilmer, "Business Involvement in Urban Problems," *Business Horizons,* June 1968, p. 16.

- Feeling of hopelessness.
- Difficulty in grasping expected discipline and social norms.
- Problems in adjusting to urban and industrial life.

Poor educational background. This is one of the principal reasons for unemployability. The hard-core unemployed who fall in this category must be educated in the subjects necessary to the basic knowledge and comprehension ability which are prerequisites to job training.

> The educational attainment which significant proportions of the long-term unemployed and poor bring with them offers a very narrow vantage point for a retraining effort. For many of them, indeed, the prescribed course first is the most basic kind of training in reading, writing, and numbers. The occupational goals are correspondingly circumscribed for substantial numbers of potential trainees.
>
> ... Job development is subject to considerable constraints when one out of every five in an obviously key group such as the long-term unemployed has not even finished elementary school.[7]

Also to be taken into consideration is the fact that there is not necessarily any relationship between the number of years of formal schooling a person has had and the knowledge and intelligence he requires to be classed as employable. The Office of Economic Opportunity has reported that 95 percent of all Job Corpsmen entering conservation centers had completed the sixth grade, yet only 13 percent could obtain better than sixth-grade equivalent on a standard achievement test.

No concept of work or training. Having never or very seldom experienced work of a rewarding nature or been given the benefit of effective training, many of the disadvantaged have very little understanding of what work or training is all about. True, the situation is not as bleak as it may first appear to be. The findings of one study state, "Planners who regard poverty-ridden individuals as lacking self-reliance and respect for the value of education might

[7] Seymour L. Wolfbein, *Education and Training for Full Employment* (New York, Columbia University Press, 1967), pp. 125, 126. This book is a very effective study of the background and some initial results of poverty programs. It contains useful basic information on the hard-core unemployed and the training problem they present.

well examine the factual support for this belief. . . . Education is desired by disadvantaged persons more than is generally realized, but . . . they often feel inhibited about stepping out of the routine in which they find themselves to secure it."[8] At the same time, the fact remains that training in what work is, how to work, what it requires of the individual, and what is involved in training must very often, like the necessary educational background, precede job training or be made part of it. The very fact that it is difficult for those who have had average or better opportunities in life to understand that people can be so deprived is one of the reasons why approaches to training the disadvantaged may lack needed realism. We must remember constantly that many of the hard-core unemployed have not had the opportunity to develop the basic habits and outlook which are normally accepted as being part of man's makeup and attitude.

> What is lacking, apparently, is not the desire to better one's self, but the awareness of what is involved in doing so. . . . The tentative hypothesis seems to be that the aims of the trainees are modest and clear, but the commitment to them is either superficial and tenuous, or complicated by competing motives. Moreover, in many cases there is no real awareness of what is required to attain the ends expressed, nor any preparation for the sacrifices and frustrations which may be encountered.[9]

Feeling of hopelessness. Being disappointed oneself, or being influenced by the disappointment of other members of the disadvantaged, has in many cases resulted in a feeling of incompetence and rejection by society, loss of motivation to try again, and an obsessive fear of failure. These factors tend to bring about withdrawal on the part of their victims, with loss of the initiative and self-respect required to begin developing traits which are needed for some degree of continuous employment. Once an individual has personally met with numerous rebuffs in looking for a job, or has heard of such experiences, the basic desire to be productive gradually

[8] William F. Brazziel, *A Study of Factors in Workers' Decisions to Forego Retraining Under the Manpower Development and Training Act of 1962* (Norfolk Division, Virginia State College, June 1964), p. 31.

[9] Lauren G. Wispé, *Attitudes and Motives of MDTA Trainees: A Pilot Investigation*, Manpower Report No. 11 (Washington, U.S. Department of Labor, Office of Manpower, Automation and Training), November 1965, p. 3.

diminishes. Many of the disadvantaged have reached the point where they have lost all sensitivity and insight; they feel neither hopelessness nor despair; thus they do not even recognize their plight or its nature. A labor department research social psychologist involved in the area of training states:

> To be convinced that the changes will be worthwhile, people must see the inducements as rewarding. Only those conditions which are convincing will have motivational impact. And here we face a vicious circle. People who have a history of social deprivation have learned to live by reduced needs and impoverished satisfactions. The "rewards" of a "better life" are to them just so many words. These people have had no direct experience with these "rewards." The hard-core unemployed might be defined for psychological purposes as those people who have had a history of motivation characterized by reduced needs and impoverished satisfactions; while, on the other hand, it is exactly these reduced needs and impoverished satisfactions which produce deprived lives.[10]

For job training to be effective with this group requires that programs include measures which will assist these victims of circumstance and environment in achieving a sense of hope. What is even more basic is that they develop the capacity for *feeling*, and to become sensitive to the reward and motivating factors which normally influence individual behavior. Only if this is accomplished can this category of the disadvantaged achieve the status of really being employable.

Difficulty in grasping expected discipline and social norms. Never having had to discipline themselves to any significant degree, and coming from an environment which has entirely different social rules and expectations, the disadvantaged find it difficult to fit into group activity or to behave in an acceptable way. Many of this group have the vocational aptitude and the basic intelligence and knowledge needed for expected performance; but, because of what society would term character deficiencies and social-psychological inadequacies, they are unable to accept supervision, are frequently absent or tardy, or have no concept of sanctioned manners and

10 Lauren G. Wispé, "Motivational Problems in Training," *Occupational Outlook Quarterly* (U.S. Department of Labor, Bureau of Labor Statistics), September 1965.

ordinary politeness. Being a product of another world with a different set of norms and behavior patterns, they naturally feel alien to and rejected by society with its fixed code of behavior. They must learn to accommodate themselves to discipline, habits, and social mores of the workplace in order that they may win the approval of their fellow employees.

Problems in adjusting to urban and industrial life. The disadvantaged who come from rural areas, as well as those from the ghetto, may be overwhelmed by the drastic change of environment they find in the business community. Life in the country or the ghetto is far removed from normal urban surroundings and from the shop or office setting. Entering this strange new world without some opportunity for understanding it and adjusting to its requirements, and for learning how to act and survive in it, can shake the little confidence and sense of security that the disadvantaged may have and result in fear of failure and a strong desire to return to the accustomed life and surroundings. Those who do remain—after undergoing the dramatic transition involved without proper preparation—often exhibit traits which appear to indicate that they are nonreceptive, uncooperative, unresponsive, and unwilling to learn. In reality, however, they are confused, embarrassed, and bewildered by their unfamiliar surroundings and what, to them, is the strange behavior of the people they come into contact with. They simply do not understand how to respond.

Developing the Proper Perspective

Success in training the disadvantaged is in large part assured when the organization recognizes the nature of the task and develops the attitude, interest, and perception which are needed to view it from the right perspective and to condition the people concerned to the many aspects of the training problem. Looking at the assignment as simply another training job will probably result in disappointment for the organization and further failure and rejection for the trainees, making their plight even worse.

The proposition under review here holds that at this juncture of our history and in the immediate years ahead the course of vocational and adult education is a matter of utmost import in the war against poverty and unemployment. It holds further that vocational education and adult education have to go beyond the provision of some overt skill endowment if they are to provide meaningful pathways for disadvantaged groups. Both also have to provide occupational education, an education about the world of work itself and other features of the American environment, as well as a vantage point for the development of motivations about and responsibilities toward that environment.[11]

Further insight in the concepts that are basic to an understanding of what the task of training the hard-core unemployed involves is implicit in the way John Rubel, vice president of Litton Industries and previously Assistant Secretary of Defense for Research and Development, viewed the operation of the Job Corps.

Rubel reasoned that the poverty program, in undertaking the Job Corps in the mid-1960's, was in much the same position that the Space Agency was in the late 1950's when it was decided to put a man on the moon. At that time, no one knew exactly what techniques we were going to use. In fact, in order to find out the best technique, highly specialized research would have to be carried out and evaluated—research which had to be consciously planned and coordinated. And in order to create a system to put a man on the moon, many different kinds of scientists would have to be brought together to work under central direction according to a plan which set out specific interim tasks, and then continuously evaluated progress and fed back the results of those evaluations into the system.

The Defense Department and the Space Agency had found that corporations with "systems capabilities" could plan and program these complex undertakings much better than a government bureaucracy. The Job Corps, Rubel argues, was just such a complex undertaking. No one knew the "right" way to run a Job Corps center. Furthermore, it would take an enormously varied array of talents to design and carry out an effective program, and then redesign it according to its own successes and failures. It would take teachers, certainly, but it should also take psychologists, psychiatrists, and doctors, and community relations experts

11 Wolfbein, *op. cit.*, p. 70.

and guidance counselors and many other kinds of specialists who would all have to work according to a system or a plan which could be tested and measured and evaluated and modified. Furthermore, every Job Corps center would have to adjust its program by making changes in many different "variable" inputs —the kinds of enrollees who were sent to the center, the infinitely different combinations of work training, education, and recreation experiences which the enrollees would be influenced by, the length of time at the center, etc.[12]

What is being stressed here is that there is much more at stake than training per se and that the situation must be viewed from the standpoint of rehabilitation and total human development.

Simply giving the disadvantaged—with some exceptions, of course—the basic knowledge to qualify for employment will not necessarily make them employable. Moreover, it will probably not insure them long-term employability. Loss of self-respect, fear of failure, maladjustment to urban life, and like difficulties also must be given adequate attention. Opportunities Industrialization Center, administered by Philadelphia's Reverend Leon Sullivan, has, in addition to teaching skills, achieved success among Negroes by incorporating in its program education in personal pride, self-respect, and motivation. In describing Reverend Sullivan's concept, *Time* magazine states:

> The students, many of them migrants from the rural South, were taught achievements of their own race and of other minorities. Not only were they told how to conduct themselves in a job interview, a basic lesson other such courses sometimes overlooked; they were also instructed in the basic urban skills— shopping wisely, handling money, attending to personal hygiene and grooming.[13]

In three years this organization has successfully trained and found jobs for 3,000 people, or 90 percent of its graduates.

A similar approach is being followed by a Los Angeles organization called Operation Bootstrap. Its program relies a great deal on

[12] Christopher Weeks, *Job Corps: Dollars and Dropouts*, pp. 98-99. Copyright © 1967 by Christopher Weeks. Reprinted by permission of Little, Brown and Company, Boston.
[13] *Time*, March 23, 1967, p. 25.

motivation training and includes instruction in Negro history, communication skills, and social adeptness. Sensitivity group sessions are administered by psychiatrists. *Business Week* reports:

> The object of the program's social side is to raise the low self-esteem of slum Negroes and to instill in them a sense of purpose and trust in their ability to help themselves. At the same time, it is intended to prepare them to handle the social aspects of the jobs they are training for.[14]

At first glance this appears to be too formidable a task—one which many business organizations may conclude is far beyond their capabilities or their proper realm of operations. True, the problem is complex and demanding, but it is no more so than many of the other challenges which have been met successfully by industry. If the systems approach is effective in achieving the technical or overall business objectives of organizations, should it not also be both applicable and useful in the area of human development?

The use of a systems approach is strongly recommended by Theodore V. Purcell.[15] Also, *Factory* magazine describes one company's program for training the disadvantaged which embodies some aspects of this approach:

> One such program, taking place over a 19-week period, was conducted during day-shift working hours by a large manufacturing company. Forty percent of the time was devoted to classroom instruction and the balance allocated to work and informal counseling (the latter taking place in the factory to orient trainees to factory surroundings and procedures). Outside consultants taught remedial reading and arithmetic; two foremen taught industrial orientation and training. Finally, informal individual and group counseling was used to support new learning and social adjustment to supervision and work rules.[16]

[14] "A Self Help Program Stirs a Negro Slum," *Business Week,* March 25, 1967, p. 67.

[15] Theodore V. Purcell, "Break Down Your Employment Barriers," *Harvard Business Review,* July-August 1968, pp. 65-76.

[16] *Factory,* August 1967, p. 14. See also James D. Hodgson and Marshall H. Brenner, "Successful Experience: Training Hard-Core Unemployed," *Harvard Business Review,* September-October 1968, pp. 148-156 for Lockheed's latest methodology; and "How to Turn Dropouts into Steady Workers," *Business Week,* August 31, 1968, pp. 64–68 for International Harvester's recent successful experience in hiring and retaining the hard-core unemployed.

Not to be discounted is the fact that the procedures and talent needed are of the kind which will be required to conduct the environmental and social research that many business leaders feel will be a prerequisite to future growth. Thus the task of getting together the necessary capabilities and developing a system that will attack the problem effectively can be looked upon as a start at structuring the foundation for environmental and social research and providing the nucleus of a new function which will grow with time in importance and service to the organization. The experience in such research—how to organize it, conduct it, and implement its findings—which should result from the undertaking should be of great value in charting courses of action requiring a similar approach and the same type of human effort.

Instituting a System

Once it recognizes the complexity of the problem and has some understanding of its many different facets, the organization is ready to begin girding itself to insure the kind of behavior, on the part of the personnel concerned, that will be needed to implement a program of action.

Top management must commit itself personally to the program and must make its commitment known and understood by the organization. Unless effort by the higher echelons of the business is exerted in the direction of gaining acceptance at all levels—but particularly among those employees who will be directly involved in the program—its chances of success are almost nil. The problem is not simply one of employing and training the disadvantaged; it is also one of training the organization to accept it and to cooperate in its implementation.

The following description typifies the methods that industry is using to insure this understanding and cooperation:

The corporate president himself, with the help of his communications staff, formulated company policy in precise and persuasive terms.

The communications staff sees to it that company house organs regularly carry articles on integration so as to build peer-group support of minority employees in departments and work gangs.

Booklets are prepared describing the careers of present minority employees, giving a "success image" not only to employees, but also to recruits.

Corporate equal employment statements are inserted into employee handbooks and union contracts.

Regular intracompany meetings or seminars are held with operating and staff supervisors (and occasionally with members of the Negro community, including militants) to discuss equal employment issues so that instead of rediscovering the wheel, managers of one unit can find out what works in another unit, what problems arise, and how to cope with the inevitable difficulties.

Company policy statements on racial employment are communicated to all employment sources, agencies, schools, and churches, as well as to stockholders, consumers, and unions.[17]

The president of American Telephone and Telegraph Company, Ben S. Gilmer, relates what his company is doing in the way of employee orientation:

As we move forward with our programs of aid in the cities, it quickly becomes apparent that we ourselves need to know more about the problems we face and about the elements that give rise to them. With this in mind, Bell System companies are undertaking what they call urban orientation programs to acquaint supervisory employees with the dimensions of the job to be done. They are also designed to develop an understanding of the Negro, his traditions, his trials, and his capabilities. Sessions include films, discussions on urban problems by leaders in the effort to solve the problems, talks by ghetto leaders, reading, and, in many cases, a visit to a blighted slum neighborhood.

Our self-educated effort includes the circulation of a series of booklets designed to spread knowledge and understanding. Titles are: "A Profile of Education in America"; "Ghetto Schools and Ghetto Youth"; "Federal Programs"; "State and Municipal Programs"; "A History of the Negro in America"; "The Black Militants—Negro Moderates"; and "Commitments of Other Busi-

[17] Purcell, *op. cit.*, p. 70. See also "Business and the Urban Crisis," a McGraw-Hill special report appearing in *Business Week*, February 3, 1968, pp. C1-C16. Both articles contain many examples of what business is accomplishing in the area of employing and training the disadvantaged, as well as other practical information on the subject. Some of the ideas in this section emanated from these two sources.

nesses." Aside from their content, these publications also indicate internally that we have definite goals and intend to pursue them. For the same reason, we are increasingly using our company periodicals, house organs, and the like to enlarge understanding. We have begun a monthly publication devoted entirely to what our companies are doing to live up to these responsibilities.[18]

The work groups to which disadvantaged trainees are to be assigned, along with their instructors and supervisors, should be given special counsel and instruction on the nature of the problems they face and the role which they can play in helping this different kind of employee surmount the drawbacks of his background and adjust to work expectations and the environment of the workplace. Having them recognize that this is a special type of person, requiring patience and understanding as well as extra effort to prevent his being humiliated and to minimize the chances of aggravating his natural fear of failure, should be an objective to strive for.

Seeking help. Training the hard-core unemployed is a problem which is still in its infancy, and not very much published information is available on the subject. Even the agencies and companies that are conducting programs admit that they are groping for answers to many questions and must resort to considerable experimentation. But some knowledge has been developed, and those interested will naturally be wise to seek it out and profit from the lessons learned by others. The Urban League, Los Angeles' Operation Bootstrap, Chicago's Christian Action Ministry, Philadelphia's Opportunities Industrialization Center, local welfare and other government agencies, and business organizations that have spearheaded this movement are possible sources of assistance and information. Personnel can be recruited from them to help set up and conduct a company program.

The National Citizen's Committee for Community Relations, Washington, D.C. 20530, has organized a taskforce service of executives who have had experience and good results in their own companies in solving problems associated with the disadvantaged and who will advise others on a voluntary basis. The organization is also distributing a regular newsletter which cites company experiences in the areas of recruiting, training, and supervising the hard-core

18 Gilmer, *op. cit.,* pp. 21-22.

unemployed and includes information on industry-related programs in education, housing, transportation, health, and welfare.

Determining involvement. How much of the total task is to be undertaken by the organization's personnel and how much should be assigned to outside agencies and consultants is a question that must be pondered in the early planning stages. The degree of involvement will depend on the qualified human resources and talent which the organization has available and can assign to the project and on the scope of its experience in similar or related undertakings. Rather than going all out from the beginning, it may be advisable to take on only part of the task and bring in outsiders to handle part of the system—for example, to teach remedial reading, arithmetic, and communication or to do the necessary counseling. After the organization has become familiar with the requisites for effective operation in the various aspects of the system, it can consider taking on more and more of the responsibility.

Since this kind of training is still a gray area so far as methodology and procedure are concerned, it will be best to start with a small, rather than a large, group of trainees. This will permit greater flexibility and maximum concentration on the individual, and it will simulate a laboratory experimental approach which can be observed more closely and be a source of useful information for future applications. Another consideration is that since most of the disadvantaged have already been victims of rejection and failure, and another such experience could completely destroy their self-confidence and make their fear of failure incurable, every reasonable safeguard should be adopted to keep them from failing once again. That the risk is less with an experimental group which can be increased in numbers as the organization gains experience, knowhow, and confidence is one of the lessons that emerges from the Job Corps.

> . . . If the Job Corps is to achieve this potential for developing new, more effective techniques for solving the most complex teen-age poverty problems, it must change its administrative priorities. In simplest terms, it needs to give far more attention to the *quality* of its effort, and far less to the *quantity*. There is little to be gained from pushing larger and larger numbers of trainees through programs of doubtful effectiveness which many of them fail to complete. There is much to be gained from putting

far greater effort into finding out what it takes to hold the enrollees in the program and what makes a successful graduate.[19]

Because of limited resources, lack of know-how, more pressing problems, or other handicaps, many organizations may not be able to develop their own programs for aiding the disadvantaged. In such cases, they can offer encouragement, cooperation, and financial help—for example, donate or lend equipment needed for training purposes—to the Urban League, Operation Bootstrap, the Opportunities Industrialization Center, and other organizations with similar purposes. They can also sponsor "street academies," usually located in slum areas, which are designed to search out dropouts and lure them into an educational program which is an informal learning arrangement with the objective of encouraging the completion of high school requirements and even college attendance.[20] Providing job opportunities for graduates of these "academies," with ample guidance and counseling until they have made adequate adjustment, is another significant contribution that many firms can make.

Moving into action. Most training programs follow the practice of selecting trainees on the basis of qualifications needed to comply with training and job requirements. In the case of the disadvantaged, the approach must very often be the opposite—design programs to fit the trainees rather than try to select trainees to fit the programs. This requires a determination of the reasons why prospective trainees are unemployable and have become members of the hard-core unemployed and the tailoring of a plan which will attack these basic causes. Parts of the program may have to be individually oriented, since there can be considerable variation in the reasons why people fall into the category of the disadvantaged.[21]

Care must be exercised in the method used to decide the status of trainees. The usual tests and testing procedures, based on the culture and language of the white man and on normal upbringing and background, are in most cases not valid when applied to the disadvantaged. Nor can a determination be reached by observing

19 Weeks, *op. cit.*, pp. 240-241.
20 See *Time*, August 2, 1968, p. 50.
21 "Increased emphasis must be placed on an individual case-by-case total approach in recruiting, counseling, training, and placement of disadvantaged youth and adults." See Wolfbein, *op. cit.*, p. 211.

behavior, for ". . . what may seem to be impenetrable ignorance and near illiteracy in a prospective worker may well be having learned to communicate in a substantially different way than that of the prospective employer or the members of the public with whom the worker may have to deal."[22] Counseling, continuous surveillance, and experience offer the only way, for the time being, to determine the reasons for unemployability and the advisable remedial action. Best able to handle this phase of the training program are professional psychologists, sociologists, employment interviewers, and former members of the disadvantaged who have learned to lead productive lives.

Establishing opportunities. Existing standards of employment may have to be lowered, and new job categories created, to provide openings suited to the capabilities of this group of prospective employees. This will require insuring understanding and acceptance of less than desirable employees on the part of supervisors and work groups. Unless this step is effectively implemented, the supervisor or the peer group will reject the substandard worker, meaning that all the company's effort will have been in vain.

For a long time jobs have been tailored to fit equipment and machinery. The task here is to fit the job to the qualifications of the worker. This may at first appear to be uneconomical, but it may provide a worthwhile experience, for indications are that more and more work will be structured according to the talents and skills of the individual employee rather than vice versa. Jobs such as "technician's helper," "electrical maintenance assistant," "nurse's aide," and the like, if carved out as starting places for the disadvantaged, can relieve knowledge workers of routine tasks and thus enable them to devote more time to the significant aspects of their work. This may really be a blessing in disguise, for it would appear that the helper or assistant category of work will become more and more essential in increasing the effectiveness of the knowledge and professional-type worker. In fact, this high-level kind of employee may very well demand that work be organized in this way.

Although the worker may have to be first employed in a low-skill job, the possibilities of upgrading and advancement should be considered in the training program in order to provide a sense of

22 89th Congress, 2nd Session, Senate Calendar No. 1680, Report No. 1712, Manpower Development and Training Amendments of 1966, October 12, 1966, p. 2.

opportunity as well as chart the path for a better future. Restricting the disadvantaged to certain kinds of work at the beginning of their employment may be justifiable in many cases, but freezing or segregating them in jobs with no future can bring about the same kind of situation within the organization that training is attempting to alleviate. Lack of formal education or polish does not necessarily mean below-average intelligence or a lack of native ability. Harry Oostdyk, director of the "street academy" project for the Urban League, argues that most slum children are shrewd, realistic decision makers, and Chicago's Christian Action Ministry operates a school for the disadvantaged which has achieved a better college-admission record than Chicago's public high schools.[23] To neglect the potential of the disadvantaged not only may lead insidiously to the formation of a "ghetto" within the company, but will almost certainly deprive the business of talents which could contribute substantially to higher-level work.

Solving personal problems. Adjustment to work, in the case of the disadvantaged, is much more complex than the situation faced by the average new employee. A completely new way of life—which is what confronts the disadvantaged worker—is a difficult situation for anyone to cope with. The work itself will possibly not present problems, but acquiring the right habits, breaking old ones, learning self-discipline, moving away from long-standing behavior patterns—all these add up to a trying task and one which requires assistance.

An excerpt from the *Business Week* report on the subject illustrates the varied personal problems which must be considered as an integral aspect of training the hard-core unemployed.

> ... The line between training and therapy gets very thin indeed. Fear of failure, for example, is widespread.
>
> "These kids are oriented to failure," says an Inland Steel vice-president, William G. Caples. For that reason, Kodak's BFE classes aim as much at instilling confidence as at teaching facts. Says an instructor: "Most of these people have failed everywhere—in school, at home, in jobs. So we try to put them in situations where they'll succeed."

23 *Time,* August 2, 1968, p. 50.

Since they fear failure, many trainees resist responsibility—at least at the start.

"We start them off where they make no decisions," says Training Department Manager R. H. Hudson of Lockheed, Georgia. "Then we slowly let them take on the responsibility."

First-line supervisors get involved in mundane problems. Stanley W. Hawkins, training coordinator at Lockheed Missiles, points out: "We help with problems, on shift and off—getting people into hospitals and out of jail, getting gas and electricity turned back on, towing cars off the freeway, fighting off finance companies, arguing with car dealers."

How do you cope with problems like these? One way is to put qualified Negroes into supervisory and managerial jobs.

"You can use some white guys, but there's a real need for the worker to identify with the top guys, the upper echelon," says Leon Woods, the 24-year-old Negro general manager of Watts Manufacturing Company in Los Angeles. This is the highly publicized company that Aerojet-General started in the riot-torn Watts area to provide jobs for Negroes in their own neighborhood. One of Aerojet's aims was to eliminate a prime cause of absenteeism—long trips between slums and plants, often without public transportation.[24]

The obstacles to urban adjustment created by rural or ghetto upbringing also demand special handling. The tenure of employment and the ability of the employee concerned to adjust to his new environment will depend considerably on the willingness of the employer to provide the help needed to facilitate adaptability to city life and new work surroundings. The personnel department and immediate supervisors should do everything possible to acquaint the worker with all that may be unfamiliar to him and make him feel at ease. This can even include helping him with banking arrangements, introducing him to the religious organizations of his preference, acquainting him with available medical facilities, and so on. The new situation must be so introduced that it will not frighten the employee to the point where he will lose confidence in his ability to cope with the challenge and be scared into returning to his familiar environment and habits.

[24] *Business Week, op. cit.*

Assembling the personnel. The needed personnel and the qualifications they should have will be determined by the extent of the
company's commitment. A complete program will require experienced counselors, as well as instructors proficient in teaching
remedial reading, writing, and arithmetic and the terminology and
communications media of the workplace. Psychologists, social
workers, job-classification personnel, and others with knowledge of
the special problems presented by the disadvantaged should be on
hand or available for consultation.

The work groups to which these new employees will be assigned
are as significant a part of the training group as any other personnel.
So are their supervisors. Not to be overlooked is the assignment of
a "buddy" to each hard-core worker to help him sustain himself
emotionally, psychologically, and trainingwise as a worker and
citizen, and to furnish guidance in solving personal problems and in
meeting the technical and social demands of the job and the new
way of life.

The buddy or coaching plan appears, in fact, to be a most
important aspect of training the disadvantaged. Jobs Now in Chicago
reports 83-percent success where buddy-type support programs
exist, whereas, in companies where no such plan is operating, only
24 percent of those hired are still working.

The first thing to accomplish is to get all the interested personnel together in a working team. Each member must recognize
his own role, as well as the part to be played by other people and
functions in the system, and each must be trained in the complex
nature of his assignment and given a sense of individual and system
responsibility to the task at hand.

Dropouts

It is only in rather recent times that dropouts have become a
problem. There have always been dropouts, but the makeup of the
job market has now reached the point where they can no longer
find remunerative economic opportunity or employment to provide
even the basic necessities. The trouble is, not so much that they did
not finish high school, but that there seems to be no chance of their
finding gainful employment in contemporary society.

Until just a few years ago, dropouts could find rewarding jobs and a place in the economy. Today, increasingly, they cannot. This rapid change of events is evidence of the new upgrading in qualifications necessary to meet the requirements of present-day jobs. And the fact that our economy can no longer provide opportunities for dropouts points to the need for greater attention to continuous training of the contemporary workforce. For, unless industry adopts programs designed to keep its employees up to date, an even more serious dropout problem may be in the offing: that is, the problem of dropouts from the gainfully employed.

The reason for our concern over the social and economic problem of the dropout—his inability to lead a productive life because of inadequate education—indicates the remedy: providing him with a type of education and training which will be lasting and serve as the basis for meeting the work requirements of the future as well as the present. Too often, training is of a stopgap type which has as its major purpose that of giving the dropout only the essential tools which will facilitate employment in the shortest possible time. This approach, although providing an immediate solution, does nothing to insure long-term employability. It will almost always result in a return to unemployment by those who have been the victims of this shortsighted course of action. Moreover, the fact that they are now older, plus the blow to their morale at having again been rejected by society and being faced with the humiliating experience of another period of forced unemployment, makes rehabilitation even more difficult.

Although the training of dropouts very often requires a social-psychological approach, it should still take into account the basic elements of training philosophy emphasized earlier in this book— if it is to have favorable long-term effects. Business should be concerned about helping this group of prospective employees achieve the status of long-term employability for many of the same reasons that it should be helping to solve the problems of the disadvantaged.

Boys and girls drop out of high school for various reasons. In some cases, it is a matter of family finances; in others, the difficulty is lack of interest. Being bored with school because it does not offer sufficient challenge can lead to the impulse to seek challenge elsewhere—and result in the termination of formal education before graduation from high school. Dropouts do not necessarily lack basic intelligence. Many have the mental ability to learn the skills they need to enable them to lead productive lives.

In still other cases, young people leave school simply because they do not fit into the group, cannot adjust to the school environment, or cannot cope with the demands made of them. This can be due to social-psychological problems, stemming from background and upbringing, or it may result from not having the elementary skills necessary to keep up with the class. For example, the average dropout is at least two years behind the norm in reading, and lack of reading ability is the principal reason that one-third of those students now starting high school will fail to graduate.

What business organizations can accomplish in this area depends, in large part, on why the would-be employee quit school. The task of rehabilitating those who terminate their education for social-psychological reasons best comes under the heading of helping the disadvantaged, and many of the suggestions previously made regarding the training and employment of the disadvantaged should be applicable. Some companies conduct or sponsor special classes to upgrade reading ability and understanding of mathematics for those who have the potential for learning a skill. And, through various kinds of public relations programs, many firms are emphasizing the necessity of at least a high school education in order to qualify for a job with a reasonable wage.

Probably the greatest service that business can render is to cooperate with the local educational system in helping potential dropouts complete their education. Where a student is likely to quit school for economic reasons, because he lacks interest, or because he cannot find sufficient challenge in school work to persevere, business may be able to provide part-time employment which furnishes the incentive required to change a potential dropout into a high school graduate. Offering such employment to a boy or girl who has the qualifications to complete high school under near-normal conditions is the least costly and the most effective way to be of assistance.

Many companies are presently engaged in this type of program, and many are finding it to be a successful venture. For example, J. I. Case Company reports that 80 percent of the participants in its program who were potential dropouts have completed high school. This is a very high percentage, even for those groups without special problems, and is therefore proof that business can make a substantial, positive contribution in this area of human development. However, participating in this kind of program requires careful thought and planning and should not be undertaken unless the organization is sincere in its intentions and determined to spend the time and effort necessary to insure its success.

Here follow some guidelines[25] for instituting and conducting such a cooperative business-school program:

- The program requires the close cooperation of the enterprise and the educational system of the community or area. Each group must be in full agreement on the importance of the project, and it must have the full support of all the personnel concerned, in both the business and the educational system. This support should not be of a token nature, but should include the strong backing of top officials of both groups.

- The general purpose of the program and the rules governing its implementation and operation should be worked out by the two parties and put in writing to insure that there are no areas of conflict, that the best possible procedures are devised, and that the possibilities of misunderstanding are minimized. It should be kept in mind that the objective is to provide the student with the incentive to advance as far as possible educationally and to impress him with the value of education in meeting present-day job requirements.

- The school system, through its counseling program, determines the number of dropouts or potential dropouts who can benefit from the program, and the cooperating business then decides how many student-workers it can accommodate. The school-work schedule is developed jointly, and methods of evaluation are devised. It is very often the practice for the supervisor to grade the student periodically and for the school system to give course credit for acceptable progress.

- The interests of the student-worker are explored by school

25 Adapted from *The School-Work Experience Program Manual*, based on the program developed by the J. I. Case Company, Racine, Wisconsin, and United School District No. 1 of Racine.

guidance counselors and company personnel so that he can be given the type of work that will offer him a challenge and contribute to his desire and ability to complete his education. Where particular talents are in evidence, the student should be assigned to work that will make use of them. He should be thoroughly indoctrinated in the purposes and objectives of the program, the work requirements, and what is expected of him. It may be advisable to have him start work a couple of weeks before the beginning of the school session to insure proper orientation to his job. All those who are directly concerned, particularly the work supervisor, should have a thorough understanding of the role they must play in the program to insure its success.

■ The cooperation of the union should be solicited. It is advisable to include stewards and other representatives in the project from its inception.

■ A most important aspect of the program is to select a proper business counselor for the student workers—a person whom the student can confide in and go to for assistance whenever needed. The counselor's job is to keep up morale; he helps the student work out problems and ease pressures which might otherwise cause him to quit school. Such a relationship requires rather close contact; but, because it is one of the key elements in the success of the program, extreme care should be exercised in selecting counselors.

■ Periodic evaluation sessions should be scheduled. These should be attended by the business counselor, the work supervisor, and a representative of the school system. It is advisable that the sessions occur with sufficient frequency at the beginning of the training period that difficulties can be spotted as early as possible—that is, before they become insurmountable. In time, sessions can be scheduled less frequently in accordance with the individual situation.

It should be apparent that this kind of program demands considerable time and sincere effort of all the participants. It should be reiterated that everyone concerned needs a firm knowledge of the task ahead, with its many complexities, before entering into it. A half-way program, or one that is not well thought out and does not retain the serious interest of all involved groups and individuals, will only result in failure and aggravate the problems of the potential dropouts and society in general. It should not be undertaken unless it has full understanding and backing.

The Bell System has many programs to aid potential dropouts in recognizing the importance of education and to help them complete high school and go on to college-level work if advisable. The program entitled "Bridging the Gap" gives special emphasis to the poorly motivated student and has been credited with preventing many of those who have been exposed to it from dropping out of school. It is described as follows:

> Parents, teachers, and local businessmen all take part in the five-phase program. It begins with summer workshops in which educators learn on company premises the skills needed in today's business world. The second phase consists of one-day sessions modeled after the summer program but held during the school year. Selected students are brought into the company during the third phase, and they see how they will fit into the adult world. This is the anti-dropout phase; the message to the students is implicit—stay in school and get a better job. The fourth part of the program sees entire classrooms on tour, inspecting equipment, hearing lectures, and talking with employees. Parents are participants in the final phase, which centers on discussion of pre-employment tests and procedures with teachers and the local businessmen who will be hiring their children.[26]

Another Bell program uses the following approach:

> At the New York Telephone Company . . . Saturday training classes in basic electricity are offered to high school students at company locations, and they lead to jobs with the company. This is a cooperative venture with local boards of education. The company will also open up its training schools for use as remedial education centers. These centers will use electronic learning equipment, which has proven to be quite helpful in upgrading individual educational levels. Trainees will be paid during the

[26] Gilmer, *op. cit.*, p. 17.

training period and, when qualified, they will be given regular work assignments with the company.[27]

Foreign Workers

The concept of the multinational corporation requires a broader outlook on training than was the case when most business was confined to domestic operations. Just as one company cannot usually adopt, in total, a training policy and program being successfully pursued by another enterprise, it should also be recognized that training practices which are effective in one country may not be applicable to the same type of operation in another geographical or cultural area. For example, it is imprudent to assume that practices which have achieved good results in the United States can be transferred wholesale to France, or vice versa; nor is it advisable to conclude that what has proved effective training procedure in France can be applied to a similar work situation in Spain.

The general conclusion on the part of many American corporations, often simply accepted without much thought or reason, that what is successful in the United States should work equally well in other countries is subject to considerable question. Rather, it is dangerous to apply policies and procedures without careful study of their applicability. The type of work and the status of the worker, the prevailing attitudes toward work and work practices in the industry and the country, and the culture and traditions of the people are the three major determinants in developing a program for training foreign workers.

> Experience indicates that American companies need to adjust training programs and even job content in order to utilize fully the capabilities of the workers they train. Ingenuity and imagination are often required to develop flexible programs to meet various social and cultural problems. American training experts have to find ways to demonstrate their respect for and understanding of persons whose cultural backgrounds, way of living, and social and religious customs are different from ours to develop the proper climate for training.

27 *Ibid.*, p. 19. The article discusses still other programs that should be of interest to many employers.

Above all, the trainers have to overcome the problem of the different attitudes toward work of people of other cultures. . . .[28]

Type of Work and Worker Status

In those nations where industry is just as advanced as in this country—for example, Western Europe—the training process described in Chapter 2-5 should be applicable. Of course, it is also necessary that the educational level be sufficient to facilitate this type of training. Because education in many countries of Western Europe emphasizes theory rather than practice, particularly in mathematics and the sciences, the product of this type of background may be even more susceptible than his U.S. counterpart to the principles of training advocated. However, in many cases the worker has not had as many years of schooling as is the norm in this country, which may make it necessary to modify training programs or first bring the employees up to a specific level of knowledge in order to institute the recommended practices. Each situation has to be studied from the standpoint of the need for training, the objectives of training, the type of work to be done, and the status of the worker.

Because of the variables which exist and the resulting difficulty of applying set procedures generally, it is hardly feasible to list detailed instructions for the training of foreign workers.

Attitudes Toward Work and Work Practices

Another factor affecting training policy and procedure has to do with the varying work practices that are prevalent in different countries. These will be accepted as quite normal by the employees, but may be looked upon as uncalled for by the parent organization. For example, the European worker is inclined to a slower work pace, and his view of his job often differs widely from that of his American counterpart.

[28] U.S. Department of Labor, *Training Foreign Nationals for Employment with U.S. Companies in Developing Countries*, Manpower Research Bulletin No. 7, February 1965, p. 1.

Serge A. Birn, a management consultant who specializes in European operations, reports as follows in *Business Week*:

> If an American worker finds that a part doesn't fit, he tosses it aside, reaches into the bin, and fishes out another part—which is exactly what he should do. To the European, it is a challenge. If you don't stop him, he'll spend the next half hour fiddling with the part till he makes it fit.
>
> He has wasted a half hour's working time. And if the product ever breaks down, the owner won't be able to get a replacement for what is really a hand-made part.[29]

Business Week also relates:

> Birn's favorite productivity horror story involves the packing department of a U.S.-owned West German machinery plant. Mysteriously, the department turned out only a third of the volume produced in the parent company's New Jersey plant. Birn discovered that the West German packers were creating works of art; cartons with gummed tape equidistant from each corner and absolutely uniform in length. It had never occurred to them this wasn't necessary and, naturally, it took time.[30]

This particular problem was solved by abandoning the time and motion studies which were used at the parent U.S. plant and which, it had automatically been concluded, should apply to the German operation. These were shelved in favor of a more specific predetermined time standards study. In addition to specifying what the workers should do, the company emphasized what they should not do. It also established pay scales based on volume so that workers were penalized financially if they spent too much time on achieving unneeded accuracy.

This case shows how established attitudes can affect work practices and points up the advisability of first determining how foreign workers look at their work before ascertaining whether training should be conducted and, if so, what training methods should be used in the effort to change those practices which may be affecting productivity unfavorably, from the American point of view. One approach is simply to give the reasons why the work must be per-

29 "Is Europe's Low-Cost Labor Really a Myth?" *Business Week*, March 11, 1967, p. 88.
30 *Ibid.*

formed in a different way and then provide incentives which will help bring about the change. This is not easy. Changing established attitudes which lead to undesirable work practices is one of the most difficult goals to achieve, and the task deserves considerable forethought. It cannot be stated too often that Americans are prone to assume, mistakenly, that attitudes are the same in other countries as they are in the United States. Studying the traditional work practices of a particular people and a particular industry is absolutely essential to determining what changes should and can be made. It is one of the chief prerequisites to structuring a rewarding training program for foreign workers.

It may be that the time, effort, and cost involved in changing work practices are such that management concludes they are best left as they are. There are, no doubt, some attitudes which are so entrenched, so much a part of the life of the people, that it would be folly to attempt to change them. Most certainly, we should guard against the temptation to try to remake the workers so that they become "American" from the standpoint of those work habits which reflect our propensity for productivity and remain "foreign" with respect to those practices and job attitudes which are superior to those of the American employee.

Tradition and Culture

Closely related to and very often the basis for attitudes are the culture and traditions of a nation. In addition to influencing people's outlook on work and the way it is done, these should play a large part in determining the applicable type of training and, more important, the training approach which must be used to produce the desired results.

For the multinational corporation, this involves much more than an understanding of the attitude toward work. Management should concern itself with people's whole way of life and their sense of values. The cultural background of those to be trained and the environment in which they have heretofore lived must be taken into consideration in order to determine what must and can be accomplished and how the established objectives can most readily be achieved. This is the case with any educational goals.

It is often the situation, as with attitude, that you cannot eco-

nomically change the outlook of the foreign worker or his sense
of values in some particular respect which may be in conflict with
American traditions or concepts of productivity. Again, this is a
value judgment that has to be made on the basis of the individual
situation. For example, in many areas of Western Europe it would
be most impractical to change the time normally allowed for the
lunch period, just as it would be imprudent to abolish the morning
and afternoon "coffee breaks" expected by certain classes of workers
in different parts of this country and regarded, not as privileges,
but almost as "rights."

The training of foreign workers is a difficult task to handle
effectively if those in charge have not been brought up in the
culture and tradition of the workers in question or have not gained
adequate knowledge of them. It can be particularly frustrating if
it is approached in the same way as is followed in training workers
for the parent organization. In those cases where the enterprise does
not have or cannot obtain employees with experience in this aspect
of training, or qualified personnel with a background in the applicable culture and tradition, the best plan is to retain the services
of a consultant who specializes in this type of endeavor. Under no
circumstances is it advisable to embark on the training of foreign
employees without experienced and qualified personnel.

9

The Challenge
to Training

ONE OF THE MOST STRIKING DEVELOPMENTS OF THE PAST 50 YEARS —increasing in momentum in recent times—is that technological innovation has come to be recognized as a major factor in organizational growth and survival. In many businesses it has become a principal objective; corporate policy commits management to its pursuit.

That a company should undertake to establish within its organization a special division dedicated to making its existing products or services obsolete, finding new products to satisfy consumer wants, and, in fact, even stimulating new desires on the part of the potential purchaser is a relatively recent concept and way of doing things.

New products, *new* industries and markets, *new* methods of making current products . . . *new* is a way of life with us today.

Take the chemical field, for instance. In any given year, 30 to 40 percent of sales are of products that didn't exist ten years ago.

Bell and Howell estimates that more than 80 percent of its current sales are from products that were not in existence even five years ago.

And DuPont estimates that more than half its current sales are from products developed during the past twenty years or so.[1]

Along with the new products come new processes. Both are creating new jobs and obsoleting what were once regarded as skills and occupations of a permanent and never-changing nature. But, more importantly, what constitutes work today is very much different from what it was ten or even five years ago. And ten years from now most job descriptions will be unlike those now in effect, even for the occupations which are presently looked upon as the most advanced and up to date.

Innovation and Work Requirements

Industry's commitment to technological innovation and its impact on work requirements are brought out rather dramatically by the "help wanted" advertisements. One corporation publicizes the following openings under the general heading of technicians:

ELECTRONIC MAINTENANCE

Will work in Plant Engineering Department. Will be required to set up and troubleshoot tape-handling equipment of electro-mechanical nature. Must be able to work independently with a minimum of supervision on preventive maintenance and calibration of tape certifiers and rewinding equipment. Must have completed high school with some college-level education in electronics. Quality control background desirable.

ELECTRO-MECHANICAL

Will perform preventive and corrective maintenance on production processing and testing equipment. Includes troubleshooting,

[1] Richard S. Reynolds, Jr., "Innovation and the Modern Manager," *Advanced Management Journal*, October 1964, pp. 29–30.

analysis, and repair of electronic, pneumatic and mechanical components.

ELECTRONIC

Will work with Engineering Department designing, building, and checking out electronic circuits. Should have some drafting capabilities. Requires high school diploma, plus post-high school education and experience in related fields.

SENIOR

Duties include setting up, tests, and preparing checkout procedures for digital tape certifiers. Will test, troubleshoot, and complete alignment of digital tape certifiers and associated equipment. Must be familiar with transistor circuits. High school and at least two years college in electronics required.

Another major corporation solicits the employment of jig and fixture builders with the following job description:

Plan the operation sequence, complete layout, machining, fabrication, and assembly of standard and nonstandard types and sizes of missile jigs and fixtures.

And a government agency advertises to fill the position of

AIRFRAMES MECHANIC

Applicants must clearly show enough competence in the following skills and abilities to perform the duties of the position: (1) knowledge of airframes mechanic trade theory, (2) ability to troubleshoot mechanical systems and components, (3) ability to assemble and dissemble aircraft components and systems, (4) ability to use measuring instruments, (5) ability to interpret mechanical blueprints, sketches, specifications, manuals, and other reference material, (6) ability to use pertinent hand and power tools, (7) ability to overhaul, repair, and test airframe components, accessories, assemblies, or mechanical systems, etc., (8) ability to do the work of the position without more than normal supervision, (9) ability to do gas welding, (10) ability to do sheet-metal work, (11) knowledge of spray-painting techniques.

From these job definitions it can be grasped rather quickly that the meaning of work and the qualifications needed for job effectiveness have undergone a significant change. The words "assemble," "follow," "put together," "fabricate," "manual dexterity," "go by a set procedure," and the like have been replaced by "set up," "troubleshoot," "work independently," "analysis," "building and checking," "testing and preparing procedures," "plan the operation sequence," and "ability to interpret." The apparent need is also for multiskill and conceptual talents. Deserving of notice is the requirement of at least a high school and very often post-high school education, signifying the value of greater knowledge, intelligence, and theoretical background. The descriptions not only imply but often spell out the independent, self-motivated, self-supervised nature of modern work.

Some observers find it convenient to dismiss these requirements as being applicable only to work demanding an especially high degree of skill or work which is not predominant in existing processes. We also hear it said often that the qualifications pertain only to those industries based on the most advanced technology. What is overlooked is that more operations are grounded in this technology than at first might appear—that its impact is in fact changing almost all kinds of work.

During the first month of 1967, the New York Sunday *Times* carried notices of employment opportunities in the following job fields:

Space systems engineer	Satellite receivers
Life support systems engineer	Mars mission and space craft studies
Digital logic design	Optical radiation analysis
Human factors science	Software technical writing
Doppler navigation	Lunar excursion module
Celestial mechanics	Re-entry aerodynamics

Some of these words were not even in the lexicon of the job field a short time ago and they reflect, of course, the accelerating innovations in just one sector of the engineering and scientific arena.

These fields have no monopoly on change, and the emergence of new jobs and disappearance of old jobs, the substantial declines in

employment in some occupations and the dramatic growth in others
are characteristic of every part of the world of work.

[Author's italics]²

The advent of the computer has all but eliminated the job of stock clerk and brought about the need for stock analysts. Where the job was once 70 to 90 percent routine standard-type work, only 10 to 30 percent now falls into this category. The stock analyst deals with exceptions to the standards; he requires a knowledge of the organization's stocking, warehousing, and overall logistics system and computer setup and the ability to assemble facts, think things out, analyze, and make logical decisions. Where there were really no significant problems for the stock clerk to handle, the stock analyst now must handle different kinds of situations that recur again and again, each demanding individual inquiry and study and a unique decision and course of action. Where only one instruction was needed to guide the stock clerk, at one government installation there are now four volumes of computer processes. And all of this is continuing to change. Almost every day brings about some improvement in the system; a new way of handling a particular phase of it or a different set of requirements calling for the reevaluation of established procedures and often the institution of a completely different and totally new system. In short, the IBM theme "Machines should work—people should think" is becoming more and more of a reality in most kinds of work.

An interview with the owner-manager of a forward-looking automobile agency discloses how even the staid job of automobile mechanic, which has been subject to very little change since the invention of the automobile, is now undergoing innovation annually, with all the complications and different demands that change involves, and is no longer the job that most people think it is.

There is not really a shortage of automobile mechanics as people claim. There are many mechanics available, but the problem is that the work which they were trained to do is no longer the same. When we think of the word "mechanic," we picture a strong right arm and a mind trained to follow set procedures. But what is now needed, because of the technological changes

² Seymour L. Wolfbein, *Education and Training for Full Employment* (New York, Columbia University Press, 1967), pp. 52–53.

which have taken place in the engine and the now numerous extras, is a much better education, theoretical knowledge, understanding, and analytical ability.

The traditional auto mechanic has discovered that he has come upon an entirely different type of work. He often does not even understand the new language of the work and is bewildered by the change. [See Chapter 2.] We tend to think that the qualifications for the job are what they were ten or even five years ago, but they have changed drastically. We have people in our shop who were well thought of as mechanics ten years ago—tops in their trade—and now they can't keep up with their work. They just can't cut the mustard.

It used to be that there were not many changes in the engine, and when there was one it was built on last year's product, and it was rather easy for the mechanic to learn the repair problems. Almost every year now we have an entirely new mechanical and electronic system in automobiles. So the mechanics have to start almost from scratch each year and can rely very little on past experience, which necessitates that they have some theoretical understanding, aptitude for change, analytical adeptness, and motivation to learn and figure things out as well as the usual qualifications. Mechanics of the old school just don't fit into this mold.

What has happened is that the work involved requires the qualifications of an instruments man rather than a mechanic. I've been thinking about trying to hire instruments men from one of the area oil refineries, but they regard their job as kind of a professional white-collar type and still look at automobile work as manual labor, with all the dirt, grease, and lower status this connotes. We're going to have to do something to get these people to understand that the job is no longer as they view it—to change our image, so to speak—so as to be able to attract the higher-caliber, better-educated, knowledge-type worker.

Significance to Training Function

Although the nature of work and the human attributes required for proficiency are undergoing continuous change, the training function in most organizations has changed very little.

What has impressed us most throughout the process of consultation with colleagues and collection of data is the near unanimity of concern that training as now practiced needs to shift gears in a major way. The consensus seems to be that there is enough dissatisfaction and also enough competence and endeavor to make significant progress in practice.[3]

In practice, training is very often behind the times instead of being in the lead and ahead of present-day demands. It frequently busies itself with attacking symptoms by instituting numerous skill-type courses, many of which are out of tune with the reality of work as it is being performed. In other cases, it is relegated to a secondary status and occupies itself with such tasks as safety training and indoctrinating workers in company benefits. It habitually responds to specific requests for assistance rather than setting long-range objectives for itself and seeking to provide the leadership and develop the training philosophy and practices which will enable the organization to keep its human resources abreast of the times.

This is not to point the finger of blame at the average training department. On the contrary, given the limited scope of its operations as defined by the organization structure and its junior status when it comes to the distribution of corporate time and resources, it has done well. What has happened is that everybody has been so busy keeping pace with the day-to-day demands of production that very little thought, time, and effort have been devoted to the type of planning and action needed to maintain and improve the company's position from the standpoint of human capital.

A new view is needed—one which looks upon the organization as an educational institution as well as a producer of goods and services. The necessity for retraining, the problem posed by dropouts, the difficulty of the disadvantaged in finding gainful employment, the prevalence of stopgap training measures and crash programs—all these emanate from situations which were predictable ten years ago. The trouble is that most managers have not viewed their businesses as being producers of human resources as well as products and services; hence the current predicament. But it seems reasonable to conclude that concepts of production management are

[3] Rolf P. Lynton and Udai Pareek, *Training for Development* (Homewood, Ill., Richard D. Irwin, Inc., and the Dorsey Press, 1967), p. xii. Reprinted by permission.

now trending in the direction of developing ways to make employees capable of continuous proficiency and able to move from one job to another. Otherwise, the organization will lose its ability to be an effective producer of goods and services. The future of work, in essence, means continuously *learning* a living.

Business has accepted the role of educator and sponsor of individual development in the case of management personnel, as is evidenced by the high priority which it gives to this function in corporate planning; it makes extensive use of internal programs and those offered by educational institutions and other outside organizations. The same forces which brought about this emphasis on management development are now operating in favor of the worker. To neglect this aspect of manpower planning could lead to a situation where the chiefs do not speak a language or operate in a way which is understood by the Indians and the lower echelons are a drag on the achievement of the purposes and objectives of the organization.

Reliance has been placed on public and private institutions (high school, trade and vocational schools, junior colleges, armed service training) to provide prospective employees with the basic background and skills which business requires. This was sufficient when there was very little change in skill makeup or job function, but such is no longer the case. Moreover:

> Unfortunately, much of what is now taught in our public schools fails to recognize that technology is generating profound changes in the nature of work. As muscle power gives way to brain power, each of us needs to understand and master, to some extent, the man-made environment about us. The heavy emphasis in the past upon verbal reasoning skills, "book learning," has unfortunately penalized those most in need of adapting to these demands, the socio-economically disadvantaged.[4]

Even when the available educational institutions are up to date in subject matter and methods, the organization will have to undertake or sponsor continuous training programs so as to enable employees to retain their proficiency. And, since the concept of total

---

[4] David S. Bushnell, "The Value of Vocational Education," in *Toward a Manpower Policy*, edited by Robert A. Gordon (New York, John Wiley & Sons, Inc., 1967), p. 198.

training is somewhat foreign to the purposes of these institutions, the employer becomes the logical provider of this kind of development.

It is now the business organization that is the creator of new knowledge in many fields, particularly in the technical areas of learning. Business is very often ahead of the academic world in terms of the resources it can devote to research and its ability to make new discoveries and find answers to long-standing problems and questions of interest. The flow of knowledge, therefore, has tended to shift direction—proceeding from the corporation and its research affiliates to the educational institutions rather than from education to business as was once the rule. And, as business delves more and more into environmental and social research, it can be expected that the same kind of switch in the direction of discovery and learning will take place in these disciplines. The point being made here is that the very nature of the development of knowledge makes for more up-to-date training under the aegis of the corporation. In a very pertinent and timely article, Neil W. Chamberlain quotes from a letter that he received from an official of a major corporation:

> In my field, geology, the majority of the new ideas are being developed within industry. There is a normal time lag of five to ten years between the development of the idea and its appearance in the periodical literature. This means that the education a young man receives is automatically antiquated, in spite of the best efforts of the professors to remain abreast of modern techniques.[5]

The corporations, at the same time, tend to continue to rely on the types of institutions which served them in the past as providers of skilled manpower—even though these institutions can no longer function in such a role as well as they did and the corporations alone are really geared to offer realistic training programs. They are not only the generators of new knowledge in an increasing number of fields but also the employers—both large and small firms—of great numbers of the educated who have the academic

5 Neil W. Chamberlain, "The Corporation as a College," *The Atlantic*, June 1965, p. 103.

background, current know-how, and vision of the future which are needed to implement modern training concepts. Almost half of those who earn Ph.D.'s every year elect nonacademic careers, and this percentage will undoubtedly rise as business increases its interest in environmental, social, and psychological research. Already the corporation is the employer of much of the most learned technical, scientific, and administrative manpower; soon it will become as well one of the principal employers of personnel who have made their mark in the liberal, social, and human areas of study.

Corporations, therefore, have no choice but to look upon themselves as educational institutions, simply because this is what they have become and what they must be to meet the requirements of the times.

> At the start, and for quite a few more years, the practical solution to the problem of retraining management properly to utilize the new technology is going to have to come from business itself. There is no hope in the immediate future that the buck can be passed along to the colleges and high schools. In time, if business truly understands what its needs are, and makes these needs known, the educational system will begin to produce young men and women trained not just to use automation equipment, but to understand its potentials.[6]

Charting the Direction

A major thesis of this book is that training must broaden its outlook and objectives in order to permit the worker to develop both the ability and the desire to make the maximum possible contribution to his work and to the organization from both the present and the future points of view. Most people want to give their best to their work, but in many situations they are prevented from being as effective as they could be because of the narrow way in which they are viewed and trained.

One goal for training to aim at is to free the employee of all possible impediments to productivity and to encourage him to expand his own resources so that he can be continuously effective

[6] John Diebold, *Beyond Automation* (New York, McGraw-Hill Book Company, 1964), pp. 80–81.

and in tune with his environment. There must first be a breakaway from the narrow objectives of job training that prevail in most organizations.

> Effective training calls, in the first place, for clarity of objectives and means. In that respect it is just like a manufacturing process. Both the ends and the means must be appropriate to the purpose. Relating them demands clear specifications for each part of the training task, including the resources of time, skill, and facilities required for it. Ensuring this is a responsibility of the first order for the training institution. Unless this task has been accomplished, a new training program is launched into a kind of void: to sail a predetermined course through an uncharted sea to an unknown goal.[7]

There must be a movement in the direction of worker training, as well as a recognition of the change in worker status from laborer and even skilled worker to professional or at least semiprofessional. There must be more to training than the devising of *programs,* as it is most often interpreted. It must become a habit, an integral part of work and a continuing part of life. Preoccupation with training based on kinds of jobs that need to be filled must now become secondary to developing the kind of people that the company and the economy are going to find necessary for effectiveness. Unless training looks upon itself in this way, and changes course accordingly, industry and the nation are flirting with the probability of increasing the numbers of people in our society who will face the same situation presently being experienced by the disadvantaged.

Much of what training must become is embodied in the "new" objectives of vocational education as formulated by David S. Bushnell, director of the Division of Adult and Vocational Research, Bureau of Research, U.S. Office of Education. He suggests that teachers—

1. Use vocational preparation as a launching pad to make general education more meaningful to practical-minded students, with stress upon the relationship between the two kinds of learning.

[7] Lynton and Pareek, *op. cit.,* p. 29. The authors use the word "institution" to mean "the place and program that offers training" (p. 6).

2. Help students to understand abstract principles by means of concrete experiences that will arouse their curiosity.

3. Emphasize manipulative, cognitive, and interpersonal skills that are common to groups of related occupations.

4. Foster attitudes and habits that will enable students to accept the responsibilities they will encounter in their jobs.

5. Show the students how they can play a role in civic affairs.

6. Offer learning experiences for a wide range of ability levels and for different backgrounds.

7. Enable students to deal with a changing labor market by developing problem-solving ability and different career strategies.

8. Promote self-reliance and self-awareness so that students can select careers appropriate to their abilities.[8]

The concepts which are being stressed, of course, involve more than simply training in its traditional meaning. To accommodate the knowledge worker and his new professional standing demands that his work be structured so that it is knowledgeable in character and professional in status.

> . . . When you look at the jobs we abolished as against the jobs we create, you will see that we are not in balance in the sense that the jobs we create will not replace the jobs we abolish. We create knowledge jobs and abolish essentially unskilled laborers' jobs. . . .
>
> We need bigger jobs, demanding jobs, challenging jobs at the beginning because, otherwise, people will acquire the habit of not producing. We need to make demands on knowledge workers because knowledge is a very peculiar resource. It degenerates incredibly fast; it is not durable. It degenerates unless it has been challenged or unless it is being added to.[9]

[8] Bushnell, *op. cit.*, pp. 202–203.
[9] Peter Drucker, "Planning for Big Changes Just Ahead," *The Personnel Administrator,* March-April 1966.

This new structuring of work goes hand in hand with training. That is, the training advocated can be effective only if the work is in accordance with training philosophy and practice, and the worker can perform as desired only if he receives the training necessary to such performance.

An important part of the overall picture is the supervisor and the way in which he handles his responsibility. He must permit his subordinates to use their knowledge and to be more independent and professional; otherwise, he will be an obstacle to their effectiveness as well as his own. What is called for is an employee-centered type of supervision or self-supervision. The role of the supervisor must be redefined, and he himself must be trained for his new and different duties.

All of this fits into the job-enrichment concept of motivation that appears to be gaining in importance and implementation. Frederick Herzberg states, "The growth or *motivator* factors that are intrinsic to the job are: achievement, recognition for achievement, the work itself, responsibility, and growth or advancement."[10] He goes on to list some beginning principles of job enrichment and the motivations involved.[11]

Principle	*Motivators Involved*
A. Removing some controls while retaining accountability	Responsibility and personal achievement
B. Increasing the accountability of individuals for own work	Responsibility and recognition
C. Giving a person a complete natural unit of work (module, division, area, and so on)	Responsibility, achievement, and recognition
D. Granting additional authority to an employee in his activity; job freedom	Responsibility, achievement, and recognition
E. Making periodic reports directly available to the worker himself rather than to the supervisor	Internal recognition

10 Frederick Herzberg, "One More Time: How Do You Motivate Employees?" *Harvard Business Review*, January-February 1968, p. 57.
11 *Ibid.*, p. 59.

F. Introducing new and more difficult tasks not previously handled

Growth and learning

G. Assigning individuals specific
or specialized tasks, enabling
them to become experts

Responsibility, growth,
and achievement

Going About the Training Job

The development of a training pattern will require, first, determination of the knowledge and learning status of the employees
and, second, the development of courses and other methods of
learning[12] which will bring those workers which the company
regards as permanent employees up to the current level of understanding required by the future scope of their work. To be de-
emphasized is the practice of attempting to base upgrading almost
entirely on specific job requirements or even on what now appear
to be the detailed qualifications that will be required for future
performance. The concept of work is in such a state of flux that it
is difficult, not to say impractical, to stress specifics in training and
to forecast future job demands in other than a general and fundamental way.

The aim should be to encourage the kind of study and learning
which will establish the foundation of understanding that will make
it possible for the worker to sense the need for change and be
capable of adapting readily to new sets of work specifics when this
becomes necessary without any, or with a minimum of, training in
these new specifics. By this is meant the development of worker
knowledge in such areas as mathematics, physics, electronics, engineering, the biological sciences, chemistry, computer science, and
so on—that is, the technological and scientific subjects from which

[12] It is not within the scope of this book to cover conventional training meth-
odology. Some recent publications in this area are: Louis Cenci, *Skill Training for
the Job* (New York, Pitman Publishing Corp., 1966); Paul M. Stokes, *Total Job
Training* (New York, American Management Association, 1966); and Bernard M.
Bass and James A. Vaughan, *Training in Industry: The Management of Learning*
(Belmont, Calif., Wadsworth Publishing Company, Inc., 1966). Rolf P. Lynton and
Udai Pareek's *Training for Development* (Homewood, Ill., Richard D. Irwin, Inc.,
and the Dorsey Press, 1967) is a behavioral approach to the subject.

work receives its direction and its impetus for change. In this way the employee should be prepared for many kinds of work that fall within the broad spectrum of his basic training.

Steps to follow include these:

1. Those responsible in the training function must determine the kinds of basic technology and knowledge and skills upon which employee effectiveness and company success are based and their applicability to continuing and future achievement.

2. The workers' knowledge and aptitude in applicable areas should be examined in order to decide which employees need to be brought up to the current level of expectations. Those who are already at the desired level of comprehension should enter the continuous phase of the training process.

3. Employees should be grouped for training purposes according to deficiencies and needs rather than by types of jobs. For example, employees who must make up a deficiency in mathematics for continuing proficiency can be brought together for upgrading in the subject, regardless of their job relationships.

4. It may be desirable, depending on the degree of expertise required, to follow up this training in basics with sessions geared to the understanding of skill techniques and their application. This can best be accomplished by grouping employees who require the same kind of skill upgrading, regardless of jobs performed. For example, many classifications of employees require proficiency in electricity, and it will clearly be more economical to bring them all together for training sessions on the subject. It will also require that instruction be broader and that electricity be treated from an overall viewpoint, enabling workers to develop a knowledge which is more flexible and more generally applicable.

5. The same sessions can also be used to develop worker comprehension of the concepts discussed in connection with introducing the worker to the job and to his environ-

ment where these have not already been included in training.

6. Time should be allotted for the improvement of communications skills (both written and oral), social skills, and work attitudes. This is particularly desirable for service jobs and types of work which bring the employee into frequent contact with the public.

7. This review of worker status can also be directed at ascertaining which work is becoming obsolete and will soon be abolished, determining the receptivity and adaptability to retraining of the employees involved, and deciding what work those workers who will find it difficult to profit from retraining can be shifted to with minimum effort and anxiety. For example, many older, less flexible workers may fit better into service or maintenance groups where general plant knowledge is as significant to accomplishment as new skills.

An example of an upgrading program is the accompanying course outline for vibration mechanics analysis, designed by the International Correspondence Schools, Scranton, Pennsylvania.[13] It can be conducted by correspondence, central seminars (gathering workers from several companies), in-plant programs, or a combination of all three. Part I of the course as outlined could include workers from occupations other than vibration mechanics who need to be brought up to date in these basic areas. Employees who need to know something of vibration mechanics in their work, even though such knowledge is secondary to their major occupation, could be included in the applicable phases of the course. Of interest is the combination of methodology—correspondence courses (depicting the trend toward self-development) plus in-plant and central seminars (indicative of a return to the classroom), all exemplifying a more formal and planned approach to training.

[13] Outlines for courses pertaining to other types of work appear in *Factory* as follows: air conditioning mechanics, June 1965, pp. 92–96; electronics technicians, July 1965, pp. 74–78; hydraulic systems, September 1965, pp. 126–129; instrument repairmen, October 1965, pp. 116–119; numerical control machine operators, December 1965, pp. 78–81; industrial optics, January 1966, pp. 108–111; welders, February 1966, pp. 64–67; in-plant communications equipment, August 1966, pp. 86–90.

Moving Ahead

Employees who have been upgraded to contemporary expectations of work understanding are now ready to join their fellow workers in the continuous-training phase of the organization's overall plan for human development. This overall plan should attempt to do more than keep workers up to date, although this should be the principal objective. Another goal, well within the bounds of realism, is to advance the education of employees as far as their abilities and motivation will allow.

> It does now seem apparent that a system of universal and life-long education will have to be devised, and there is some question whether the traditional university or college is the place to do it. It may be that among other of its new responsibilities, business will also have to put its enormous talents and resources to work educating minds, with the same enthusiasm with which it has produced goods.[14]

Those workers who have the basic aptitudes and have not completed high school should be enrolled in a plan which will enable them to do so or achieve a recognized equivalent status. This group, along with the high school graduates, should then be afforded the opportunity to complete junior-college-type courses and, if they have the ability, be encouraged and assisted financially to go on to even more advanced education.

All this is in the worker's interests, but also to be recognized is that much of modern-day work already requires a junior-college background and that this is an accelerating trend. Organizations that permit, encourage, and guide the continuing education of their employees, on company time and with company resources, will therefore find that such a policy is in point of fact very much in their own interests.

> Is it too farfetched to imagine that our major corporations might begin appointing vice presidents in charge of education, not job

14 Don Fabun, *The Dynamics of Change* (Englewood Cliffs, N.J., Prentice-Hall, Inc., 1967), Part I, p. 32.

Course Outline

Vibration Mechanics Analysis

As appearing in *Factory* (now *Modern Manufacturing*), April 1965; reproduced here by courtesy of International Correspondence Schools

Part I: Prerequisite Studies

A. Mathematics
  (a) Practical Arithmetic
  (b) Formulas
  (c) Practical Geometry and Trigonometry
In-plant: 30 hours*
Correspondence: 85 hours
Central seminar: 20 hours*

B. Physics
  (a) Matter and Energy
  (b) Laws of Motion
  (c) Velocity
  (d) Acceleration
  (e) Weight and Mass
  (f) Nature of Friction
  (g) Force
  (h) Heat
  (i) Electricity
  (j) Sound
In-plant: 42 hours*
Correspondence: 119 hours
Central seminar: 28 hours*

C. Machine Sketching
  (a) Sketching Parts
  (b) Finish Marks
  (c) Dimensioning
  (d) Partial Sections
  (e) Conventional Symbols
  (f) Graphical Presentation
In-plant: 6 hours*
Correspondence: 18 hours
Central seminar:

Part II: Vibration Analysis

A. Theory of Vibration
  (a) Vibration Defined in Terms of Machine Performance
  (b) Characteristics of Vibration
  (c) Significance of Characteristics to Analysis

In-plant: 6 hours*
Correspondence: 18 hours
Central seminar: 4 hours*

B. Detection and Measurement
   (a) Identifying Vibrations
   (b) Vibration Tolerances
   (c) Critical Valves
   (d) Instruments Available
   (e) Use of Instruments
   (f) Use of Charts
   (g) Recording Data
In-plant: 6 hours*
Correspondence: 28 hours
Central seminar: 4 hours*

C. Common Causes of Vibration
   (a) Looseness
   (b) Unbalance
   (c) Misalignment
   (d) Eccentricity
   (e) Summary of Causes
In-plant: 6 hours*
Correspondence: 18 hours
Central seminar: 4 hours*

D. Vibration Control
   (a) Isolation
     1. Methods
     2. Materials
     3. Applications
In-plant: 4 hours*
Correspondence: 10 hours
Central seminar: 3 hours
   (b) Balancing
     1. Static Unbalancing
     2. Dynamic Unbalancing
     3. In-place Balancing
     4. Single-plane Balancing
     5. Two-plane Balancing
In-plant: 9 hours*
Correspondence: 24 hours
Central seminar: 69 hours total

* The time indicated above represents the actual time spent in instruction. This time should be supplemented by outside assignments.

training in the old sense, but genuine honest-to-goodness education, and that youngsters entering the job market might select one company over another, or one community over another, because it offered them superior educational facilities? Is it too fanciful to conceive of job seekers poring through corporate course catalogues with an interest at least equal to that which they might now give to a statement of wage policy, working conditions, and fringe benefits?[15]

The cost will not be out of pocket, for most large and many smaller businesses have the needed talent to develop, schedule, and teach university-type courses. When the changing demands of worker knowledge and capabilities are viewed realistically, cost really falls into the category of investment in human capital. The only major problem is one of organization. Smaller companies, or divisions of larger ones, that do not have human resources to call upon should be able to pool their efforts and develop an area approach which should be successful in achieving the desired objectives.

Another way is to develop educational plans in conjunction with nearby institutions of higher learning. One such program designed to train aerospace electronics technicians calls for 8,000 hours of paid training and 700 hours of related evening classes at cooperating junior colleges in four years. The goal is to produce multipurpose technicians who are knowledgeable in both the theory and the practice of several fields and related areas—research and development projects, production techniques, component testing, advanced electronic systems, circuit adjustments, and maintenance. The college classes emphasize higher mathematics, electronics, materials engineering, electronic circuits analysis, instrumentation, DC theory, and radar principles. In the fourth year the student employees have courses in atomic energy, computer sciences, lasers, and masers. The work is arranged so that participants can enroll in regular junior-college courses and gain the broadening benefits attributed to association with regular students. By taking courses in social science during the summer, they can qualify for an associate-of-arts degree.

15 Neil W. Chamberlain, "The Corporation as a College," *The Atlantic*, June 1965, p. 104. Copyright © 1964, by The Atlantic Monthly Company, Boston, Mass. 02116. Reprinted with permission.

Looking to the Future

The objectives of the training function should be geared to the organization, direction, and administration of the development of human resources throughout the business in the broadest sense rather than simply the conduct of courses, many of which (like safety training and indoctrination in policies and procedures) may be important but do very little to enhance the value of human assets on a continuing basis. Training must also break away from the rather closeted view it has traditionally taken of itself; it must participate in the fundamental thinking of the organization and be willing to utilize the best talent available to accomplish its numerous objectives.

The tendency of many training departments to view their task from such a narrow standpoint that they attempt to keep the training function entirely within their jurisdiction can only lead to the usurpation of their responsibility and authority by other elements of the organization. It will result in training which is not as productive as it could be. The training department of a major installation of one large corporation, for example, conducts 500 courses with only 14 instructors, all of whom are employees of the department. Yet 5 percent of the personnel at the installation have the Ph.D., and another 15 percent have master's or bachelor's degrees. It is doubtful whether so few instructors can carry the full load of teaching of so many courses as effectively as would be the case if qualified plant personnel were utilized.

Regardless of how the training function is set up, it will have to cope with the varied aspects of life which affect individual contribution to human endeavor.

Children growing up today face a future without a Promised Land. If they are to develop a sense of themselves and of their own worth, they will have to develop an ethic of change. They will have to accept, as continuing, the changes in technology, institutions and objectives which have outmoded the Technological Program; they will have to identify themselves instead as those who trust themselves to the here-and-now, who start from where they are, who experiment, who seek the metaphors for the future inherent in their traditions, who permit freedom to change, seek new visions and become. [16]

Facilitating adjustment to the changing challenges to personal well-being created by new circumstances within and without the organization will be a growing problem for society. The older workers, the dropouts, the disadvantaged—victims of the shift from physical dexterity to mental competence and judgment as major qualifications for performance—are examples of the existing situation. And, in addition, already on the scene is the question of the effect on people of increased leisure time.

> We have in our society, at the present time, almost no concept of training people (other than the children of the wealthy) for a life of leisure. . . . We are on the threshold of a time when leisure is at last possible for most people in our society, and we are doing almost nothing to prepare them for this new dimension of human life.[17]

All changes in work and its environment, as well as all conditions which can affect productivity and the status of human expertise, will have to be more and more looked upon as fundamental concerns of training in business and industry—not only because it is in the interest of business organizations to include training in their role but, more importantly, because business and industry would seem to constitute the segment of contemporary society most able to pursue the goal of insuring the human adaptability that is increasingly necessary to contend with one's work and one's surroundings.

[16] Donald A. Schon, *Technology and Change* (New York, Delacorte Press/A Seymour Lawrence Book, 1967), pp. 217–218.
[17] Fabun, *op. cit.*, Part V, p. 21.

INDEX

Index

199

About the Author

BERNARD J. BIENVENU is professor and head of the Department of Management at the University of Southwestern Louisiana, Lafayette, Louisiana. He was graduated from the University of Southwestern Louisiana, received his Master's and Doctor's degrees in business administration from the Harvard Business School and also studied at the Universities of Paris and Lyon.

Dr. Bienvenu is president, former vice president, and program chairman of the Southern Management Association; former program chairman, vice president, and president of the Southwest Management Association; member of the board of the Louisiana State Department of Commerce and Industry; and director and vice chairman of the Evangeline Pepper and Food Products, Inc.

Dr. Bienvenu has contributed to five books, and his articles have appeared in numerous business journals.

DEC 02 1989			

HIGHSMITH   45–226